FROM SLAVESHIPS TO SCHOLARSHIPS

THE PLIGHT OF THE AFRICAN-AMERICAN ATHLETE

CHARLES PINCKNEY

authorHOUSE®

AuthorHouse™
1663 Liberty Drive
Bloomington, IN 47403
www.authorhouse.com
Phone: 1 (800) 839-8640

Published by AuthorHouse   11/12/2018

ISBN: 978-1-5246-9391-6 (sc)
ISBN: 978-1-5246-9389-3 (hc)
ISBN: 978-1-5246-9390-9 (e)

Library of Congress Control Number: 2017908394

Print information available on the last page.

Any people depicted in stock imagery provided by Thinkstock are models, and such images are being used for illustrative purposes only. Certain stock imagery © Thinkstock.

This book is printed on acid-free paper.

ACKNOWLEDGEMENTS

First and foremost, I must thank my wife Elizabeth. She inspired me to read more which enabled me to write this exciting hybrid book: part history, part sociology, and part current issues. Next, I must thank Taylor and Jordan, my treasured daughters, who valued my desire to write this book. I would like to personally thank Nicole Palacios, my first research student from the University of North Carolina at Charlotte, for her patience and commitment during the initial research stages of outlining this book. Nicole, your efforts were truly exceptional. To Walter Lee, my second student researcher, you were tremendous; you were able to jump into the game and help advance the book in a positive manner. The amount of time and research offered to me by Nicole and Walter was truly remarkable. Nicole's and Walter's suggestions, criticisms, and persistence as young scholars kept me well grounded. I was blessed to have two terrific young scholars who valued my efforts to create this book and tell a very compelling story. Tevent Wiggins, thanks brother for such a powerful book cover. You took my title and matched it up with a brilliant book jacket that captures the essences of the book title: *From Slave Ships to Scholarship: The Plight of the Black-Athlete*.

I'd also like to thank everyone who took time to let me share the concept of this book and the three athletic angels who agreed to be interviewed for this book. The interviews were personally rewarding for me, and I learned so much from Mr. Moore, Mr. Williams, and Mr. Burch. Finally, I must thank all of my students, friends, and extended family members who supported me in writing this book.

I hope that you enjoy reading it.

Best regards,

Charles Pinckney, Ph.D.

TABLE OF CONTENTS

PREFACE

The year was 2008, my first time attending the National Collegiate Athletic Association (NCAA) convention. The convention is the foundation for all NCAA business. At this convention, two special forums were planned. The first, entitled "Emergence of Excellence, a Celebration of the Rich Tradition of Intercollegiate Athletics at Historically Black Colleges and Universities," focused on the achievements of historically black colleges and universities and their students and student-athletes. There were six panel participants: Rochelle Stevens is a former Morgan State University track and field student-athlete. Olympic Medalist Mamie Rollins is a former track and field student-athlete from Tennessee State University and two-time Olympian. Jackie Slater is a former Jackson State University football student-athlete, nineteen-season veteran of the National Football League, and member of the Pro Football Hall of Fame. Doug Williams is a former Grambling State University quarterback and the first black quarterback to win a Super Bowl. Harry Carson played in the NFL for thirteen years, including an appearance in Super Bowl XXI with the New York Giants, and is a member of the College and Pro Football Halls of Fame. Willis Reed led Grambling State to an NAIA men's basketball national title before Grambling joined the NCAA and is an accomplished NBA player, general manager, and member of the National Basketball Hall of Fame.

The second session focused on the need for coaching diversity. Then-President Brand moderated a session with Gene Smith, athletic director at Ohio State University and an African American; Dr. Nancy L. Zimpher, former President of the University of Cincinnati and a white woman; and William Rhoden, columnist for the New York Times, author of *Forty Million Dollar Slaves,* and an African American.

In 2007, there were only eight black Division I football coaches and only a handful of black basketball coaches at major white universities. I knew at that point that I needed to write this book, and I had the opportunity to talk with William Rhoden briefly after the panel discussion. I shared with Rhoden how much I admire his most recent work, *Forty Million Dollar Slaves*.

My first thought was to write a paper entitled "From Slave Ships to Scholarships," not a book. At first, I feared being discredited and chastised by both blacks and whites who seem to be in denial about the current state of Negro Sports and the psyche of the modern-day black athlete. This book is my attempt to revisit and update some of the critical points William Rhoden raises.

INTRODUCTION

By some accounts, 500 years ago our African ancestors were running from the slave catcher and slave ships to avoid slavery. Today, the descendants of slaves are still running: running, jumping, shooting baskets, and catching odd-shaped balls for their masters. Blacks dominate such sporting events as track and field, football, and basketball. On any given Saturday afternoon at majority white institutions, the black athlete can be found entertaining not only their immediate white master, but also a disproportionate number of white fans, including faculty, staff, and college administrators. This, in itself, has condemned far too many black athletes to slavery and the conditions of modern-day slavery in the name of athletics. Truly, sports in America today have psychologically damaged the black athlete.

Indentured servitude or athletic slavery, it is all the same at the end of the day. Of course, we should not be referring to student-athletes as indentured servant or slaves. The NCAA is far too intelligent for that. The NCAA prefers the term *student-athlete* and has established rules and regulations that prohibit any form of compensation except for student aid that is solely controlled by the respective NCAA member colleges or universities. The term sounds much better than either indentured servant or slave. Millions of dollars are flowing into colleges and universities annually because of student-athletes. Consider it an investment for an even greater pay off. By classifying "student-athletes" as such, the NCAA and the presidents of our major colleges and universities are not obligated to pay their highly skilled physical gladiators for their services, including practice time, game time, pregame and postgame activities.

The racial appetite in sports continues to be very healthy for both black and nonblack consumers. More and more black athletes enter college with the hope of one day joining the professional ranks. For many the lifestyle not only reshapes them as a black athlete, but it conditions them to a life of constant dysfunctional behaviors. Many forms of street culture have now encroached onto many of our well-known historically white college and universities, where blacks were prohibited as students prior to the 1960s. We must not forget that we are talking about less than sixty years ago. To say that there has been a changing of the guard is truly an understatement. For example, many of today's black student-athletes are sporting tattoos, earrings, cornrow hair styles, while showcasing their unique cultural reflections.

Of equal of importance is that one is really hard pressed to find clean-cut black athletes in college today. A pervasive subculture within intercollegiate athletics has become all too common, where tattoo branding, earrings, and dreadlock or cornrow hairstyles now appear to be the norm. In many cases the tatted up black athletes and their challenging lifestyle behaviors and choices are more than likely to result in negative consequences, despite all of the significant monetary advancement garnered by some blacks in sports.

John Hoberman wrote that sports in America have psychologically damaged the black athlete and have preserved the myth of race. Has the college athletic arena suddenly turned into a new form of modern-day slavery? Are young black boys and girls being subjected to slave behaviors under the watchful hand of college athletic departments? The black athlete has been reduced to the status of a "thing or object" by its owners and consumers. Owners and consumers continue to display a grand passionate love for the black athlete. Attractive features of the black athlete include their physical, rhythmic bodies and their eagerness to entertain paying white fans in a landscape they have been allowed to dominate with their physical skills. Some may contend that the black athlete has done harm to himself by willingly participating in sports, and that black athletes have willingly enslaved themselves as a result of their athletic success and high-profile status in the black community. So the rhetorical question is this: Are professional black athletes today really million-dollar slaves with selective privileges? Are young black college student-athletes warming up in our major universities or athletic training institutions in an intensively controlled environment?

The old saying goes, if much is given, much is expected. This is no more evident than when it comes to the black athlete. Many of these million-dollar professional and college athletes are shown to have tons of stress, and many lack cognitive and psychological skills to understand the game inside the game. Being a high-profile, highly successful black athlete making a million dollars a year can be very stressful. On any given day, if you ask young black boys what they want to become when they grow up, they will tell you a professional athlete or rapper. I, too, am guilty: Growing in the rural south as a typical athlete talented enough to attend college on a possible sport scholarship, I thought that I would one day become a professional athlete. Fortunately, I received the wise advice of Dr. Elizabeth Bethel at then Lander College in Greenwood, South Carolina, during the fall of 1983; she sat me down in her office one afternoon and lashed into me about a paper I had written. Dr. Bethel broke it down to me in a way that no one had ever done before. I had enjoyed a good ride through sports for nearly a decade dating back to middle school. Dr. Bethel told me that I was not going to be a professional player. I needed to make a choice, basketball or academics. The exact words of Dr. Bethel was: "you can stay with the basketball team as the third-string point guard and continue to put forth half ass work in the classroom and put forth all your efforts in sports." This was by far the most honest conversation any adult had ever had with me. Bethel is a white woman who always had plenty to say and, for the most part, was always on point with her comments or remarks. Needless to say, after a day of thinking long and hard, I decided to clear out my locker and divorce myself from the basketball team.

That courtship between the black male athlete and sports is well documented. The main areas where blacks can achieve success are sports and music. The vast majority of young black athletes view sports as their quickest way out of a bad social situation and an opportunity for upward mobility. This is unfortunate, but it is the reality for many young black male athletes. Many complain about a lack of positive black businessman in their communities and in the media. It is equally important to note that impressionable black athletes consume countless hours of sports via media outlets. What they see over and over is older black athletes dominating sports, like football and basketball, at the college and professional levels. There is nothing wrong with being a or wanting to become a professional athlete. However, there is something wrong with being a conditioned and controlled black athlete. "Souled Out" is how Shaun Powell describes the contemporary black athlete. The black athlete has souled out on all levels according to Powell. He further notes that people with athletic background have also souled out. It is well documented that blacks from disadvantaged communities continue to be souled out on the college and professional levels if they make it professionally.

From Slave Ships to Scholarships: The Plight of the Black-Athlete provides specific themes and a set of conceptual frameworks critical to understanding the overall psychology and nuances of the black athlete, both past and present. This book offers a comprehensive look into the lives of the black athlete, the psychological struggles both on and off the field. This book draws on personal observations of various black athletes, as well as other scholars' fieldwork and scholarship.

Chapter 1 provides a brief look into the beginnings of sports within the black community, back to the colonial period. This chapter also identifies parallel characteristics of sports popular among blacks and slavery. In doing so, this chapter explores in depth the relationship between plantation slavery and the culture of sports both past and present. This chapter also explores and discusses African sports, plantation sports, college sports, and professional sports. "From Slave Ships to Plantations and Now Scholarships" thoroughly investigates the dimensions of the black athlete.

Chapter 2 consists of a actual conversation with three black sports angels and pioneering heroes from the past who offer a contemporary narrative of sports. First, there is Jackie Moore from the 1950s, one the first blacks to play in the National Basketball Association (NBA). The second is Jim Burch, one of the first blacks allowed referee college basketball games in the South at traditionally white colleges. The third and final is George Williams, one of the winningest track and field coaches in the history of the sports. Williams was selected to coach of the U.S. Men's Olympic Track and Field Team at the 2004 games in Athens, Greece.

Chapter 3 explores whether or not there is a future for the black athlete in intercollegiate athletics. This chapter provides an in-depth analysis and review of black athletes and their psychological courtship with intercollegiate athletics. It also explores the complex experience of black athletes at predominately white institutions. This chapter also calls into question the practices of historically white colleges and universities concerning black athletes and how these institutions are treating their "Cash Crop."

Chapter 4 explores how the black athlete impacted mainstream American culture. This chapter also examines the role blacks athletes have within society and the common perceptions that most black athletes are given. The scarcity of black coaches through whom to explore the issues of race and class is also be discussed.

Chapter 5 explores the academic problems associated with intercollegiate sports. Is the *student* aspect of being a student-athlete being forgotten? Are black athletes being provided with the tools necessary to succeed in life outside of their sport? This chapter also identifies issues that arise in the classroom for these student-athletes and questions whether they are receiving a proper education.

Chapter 6 revisits the "Forty Million Dollars" theory by analyzing sports columnist William Rhoden's account of the similarities between the modern-day athlete and the African slave. This chapter reflects briefly on the thoughts of sports-sociologist Harry Edwards to further the discussion.

Chapter 7 discusses the historical significance of historically black colleges and universities (HBCUs) by asking whether HBCUs are playing a game beyond their abilities. This chapter also explores HBCUs' rich history and their unique learning experience for black students. This chapter also examines the resource and funding limitations affecting top-tier athletic programs at the HBCU level and explores possible solutions to improve HBCU.

Chapter 8 takes the reader on a journey in the history of black women and sports. How have black women been able to break ground as athletes? How has the black women athlete gone on to successful careers in athletics despite the limited opportunities? How have black women athletes made significant contributions to and progress in the world of sports?

Chapter 9 tours a talented group of black women sportscasters. Similar to Chapter 8, this chapter acknowledges some of the black female pioneers in the sports world and their struggles. This chapter will examine how these female sports professionals, not professional athletes for the most part, are major players behind the microphone.

Chapter 10 is focused on the current hot-button topic in the sports world: the gay black athlete. Within the past few years, there has been a rise in the number of professional athletes coming out as gay. This chapter further explores how this dynamic impacts the athlete, their teammates, and the public.

CHAPTER ONE

From Slave Ships to Plantations and Now Scholarships

"Niggers play football, baseball and basketball while the white man cuttin' off their balls ... Niggers tell you they're ready to be liberated, but when you say 'Let's take our liberation,' niggers reply: 'I was just playin'.'"

—The Last Poets, *Niggers Are Scared of Revolution*

Let's for a brief moment think back in history nearly five hundred years and revisit the time when the first Africans were captured, packaged, and delivered to America to fill the void of essential laborers for whites. The history of slavery is an extensive timeline that includes hundreds of years of African culture infused with the growing American social structure through the Civil War. This long tradition of overseas trade transported generations of black Africans against their wills across the Atlantic Ocean to America to serve as laborers. The formation of African slavery would create an institution that would last hundreds of years.

The perception of American slavery, within the context of the modern world, consists of an accepted point of view contrived from numerous historical writings, publications, and even theories proposed by leading world scholars. In putting things into proper context, the American public has placed blacks in a class defined by the labor that they did and currently do, demonstrated by how they are socially treated and valued.

It is important to note that blacks held a unique legal status, which was inherent due to the social confines of slave institutions in which slaves endured social maltreatment, ruthless punishment (which included rape), and separation from loved ones—all in the name of capitalism.

Within the context of many plantations, there was a strong desire to mentally escape the treatment that they encountered daily. One of the primary ways of escaping the negative daily experiences associated with slavery was to develop recreational activities and outlets. In addition, it is equally important to note that not all slave owners treated their slaves equally harshly.

From the very onset, slavery was an evolving institution that experienced vast changes over generations. African slavery transformed into American slavery, and with this shift came new cultural foundations. Accordingly, traditions developed in exchange with the interactions and progression of a new cultural and social institution. It was through specific cultural development of leisure activities, such as sports, that slaves were able to establish and experience a release of anger and frustration. Recreation and sports provided the slave with a brief sense of independence from the slave identity, contrary to popular perceptions that seemingly defined slaves in a common manner of total enslavement, both mentally and physically. The representation of being enslaved was manufactured by institutions of slavery, which presented generalized stereotypical images that continue to obstruct the reality and complexity of one's actual existence as human being versus a thing or a piece of property.

Today, sports can be viewed as a modern-day, sophisticated athletic arena based on laborers and a labor system that is deeply rooted in the institutions of slavery. The black athlete laborer is part of a state-of-the-art institution. Black athlete laborers in specific sports that blacks dominate earn large salaries, drive big cars, and live in huge homes, but the owners of the institutions who control the black athlete laborers amass even larger incomes based on the institutions' values. Take, for instance, the Los Angeles Lakers and New York Knickerbockers; according to *Forbes,* the Lakers are the wealthiest NBA institution. As of 2009, the Lakers were worth a reported $607 million. The New York Knicks came in second at $586 million, while the Chicago Bulls rounded out the top three at $511 million.

Can you imagine making $1 million a year simply to play a game? Many people are quick to say that professional athletes really do not deserve all that money. Here is a quick fact to consider. The profession of teaching is one of the most economically important occupations in the world, but teachers are paid immensely less than the average, or even low-level, professional athlete. Near the end of Kobe Bryant's career, every basket he scored represented $37,940.00, which is close to the average annual salary of a classroom teacher. If he scored just two baskets in the first two minutes of the game, he would have earned more in two minutes than the average American family for one year. For those not ready for the NBA, there is the NBA's Developmental League. Kobe Bryant's last contract paid him a league-high $30.5 million per year. Breaking it down by the numbers, Bryant made almost $20 million more than the entire NBA Development League together. The NBA Development League is made up of 18 teams and a total of 280 players. In the NBA Development League, younger players make about $18,000 per year. All players are eligible for health insurance during the six-month season, receive a modest per diem, and are offered housing packages. Experienced former NBA professionals who were demoted to the Development League can earn as much as $30,000 per season.

In football, the earning and enormous contracts are also off the charts. Did you know that Aaron Rodgers ($40 million), Matthew Stafford ($31.5 million), Tom Brady ($31 million), and Matt Ryan and Joe Flacco ($30 million each), all white quarterbacks, are among the 10 highest paid athletes in the world. The picture is somewhat different for NFL rookies. The average minimum salary is roughly $420,000. If you are not good enough for the NFL, there is a lower-level league. The Arena Football League players often work part-time at other jobs to supplement their earnings, which is around $830 per game. At one point, the average Arena Football League player earned only $400 per game. The season is usually no more than 18 regular-season games. In fact, many of the players' salaries are less than $15,000 per year. Another option would be the Canadian Football League, where the average salary is about $50,000 per season.

The common misunderstanding is that all athletes are millionaires, however, the truth is that only a few real superstars like LeBron James, Drew Brees, and Alex Rodriguez are making the millions. The vast majority of athletes pull in far less, in fact many are not around their respective leagues long enough to accumulate the millions like a Kobe Bryant, LeBron James, Drew Brees, and Alex Rodriguez. Out of all of the big five major leagues, NBA players have the highest average career earnings overall.

It is important to note that not all professional athletes are earning millions. The majority of minor league baseball players continue to dream about the contracts of players like Alex Rodriguez. Many of them must live in small apartments, and the gap between the highest and lowest paid players continues to expand. In fact, many professional athletes make close to nothing or even less than that when you include the cost of living and other expenses. Alex Rodriguez earns the same amount of money annually as it would take to feed the nation's poor.

Other professional sports where athletes are less likely to become millionaire include minor league baseball, hockey, lacrosse and soccer. While major league baseball enjoys billions in revenues, there is an unadulterated cultural divide between the major leagues and the minor leagues. Minor leaguer baseball players do not have the protection of the Players Union. Some earn no more than $3,000 per season, and receive on average $25 per day for food. At the major level, players receive on average $100 per day for food. The National Hockey League minimum salary is tops among the four major American sports; however, for the minor league players, the pay is not so attractive. For example East Coast Hockey League rookies earn a minimum of $415 per week and veterans make only on average $460 per week over the course of a hard-hitting 72-game regular season. The indoor National Lacrosse League only pays about $9,200 for all rookies. It is very common for teams to load up on younger players in an effort to keep payroll low. Similar to Arena football, Major League Lacrosse will pay its players between $10,000 and $25,000 per season. The majority of the league's players work day jobs to supplement their low salaries. Many may not know that some of the richest athletes on the planet are soccer players. Cristiano Ronaldo and Lionel Messi each earn more than $50 million a year. However, in major league soccer, salaries aren't as excessive; the league minimum is capped at $35,125, and the average player salary is around $160,000. The whole professional athletic system, which allows a select group of individuals to drown themselves in money is seemingly ludicrous.

American slaves, in reality, were valued for their labor skills and devalued as humans because of the color of their skin. They were largely viewed as property like horses and cows on a farm. To create a life of human existence for themselves, slaves on southern plantations continually developed ways to escape from materialization by participating in sports and recreational activities. The traditional view of American slavery presents a dramatic image of devastation and anguish even today. Through the study of history, we learn that slavery was initially considered an economic institution within the context American capitalism.

The Slave Ships

Since the beginning of the institution of slavery, physical harm and control had been a part of the process. Slave traders would travel to the African coast, where they would hunt African tribes and capture, chain, ship, and then sell them as slaves. The Middle Passage produced a dark period in history where the number of trafficked Africans would reach beyond the hundreds of thousands. Many writers have argued that it was a sin of the South; truth be told, it was the sin of a nation. Nevertheless, slavery reflected a much broader perception, participation, and exploitation that resulted in huge profits for slave owners. The conditions on slave ships were quite alarming and undesirable; it was an insult to all humanism that any human would be treated this way. The cargo consisted of native African men, women, and even children packed ready to be sold in the South.

It is estimated that some fifteen million Africans were captured and transported to the Americas between 1540 and 1850. To maximize their profits, slave merchants carried as many slaves as was physically possible on their ships. By the seventeenth century, slaves could be purchased in Africa for a little as twenty-five dollars and sold in the Americas for as much as $150. After the slave trade was declared illegal, the price increased.

The journey from Africa generally took about two months, depending on the conditions of the sea. Those who could not escape enslavement were taken from their homeland with no clue as where they were headed. On average, each was afforded only seven square feet aboard the slave ship. As they were put onto the ship, they saw other Africans coming on board, but they were all placed into holds with virtually no contact. This situation continued day and night until there was no sight or sound of their native land. Mentally, many enslaved Africans found death was more desirable than life. Historians remind us that in the Middle Passage, many Africans jumped ship and died at sea, while other Africans carefully planned efforts to disrupt the journey to the Americas. Several slave ships burned and blew up; many Africans engaged in behaviors that resulted in their deaths.

Additionally, it was not uncommon for the white headmen of the ship, or any of the common white sailors, to have sex with African women while the men remained chained in the holds. It is important to note that the white crews of the slave ships also suffered unusually high death rates.

Running from capture was the beginning of the race for many blacks who now see slavery as a thing of the past. A significant percentage of slave deaths took place on the African coast when the slaves were being forced into the ship's hold. There were constant random attacks of diseases and sicknesses that caused mayhem at sea. There were more than three hundred voyages, resulting in many violent incidents on the African coast.

The Plantation Sports Culture

Sports have been around since ancient civilizations, and with the development of different societies came the development of different sports. African tradition, European tradition, and ultimately American tradition would construct an assortment of different styles, rituals, and customs within the complex evolution of sports.

The South's plantation culture helped to create a demand for slaves; wealthy Northerners were more than happy to use their ships and wealth to trade in slaves for profit. Recreation and sports activities quickly became an outlet for newly enslaved Africans to establish their individuality. Sports also provided the opportunity for the communal and individual events needed for mental survival.

Most slave owners sought to keep their slaves under rules regarding all aspects of life, including recreation and sports. For the most part, slaves lacked the proper gear and settings to participate in certain sporting or recreational activities. From the vantage point of the slave owner, recreation was not important; therefore, he made no real provisions for the slaves.

In fact, the slaves were rarely given the opportunity to participate in individual events without the consent or supervision of the slave owners or overseers on the plantation. Slave owners always maintained strict conditions that limited individuality and the social development of African culture. For slaves, sports provided an outlet to release built-up emotions and frustrations.

Sports also permitted them the opportunity to escape mentally from the physical realities of slave life, if only for a short period. The athletic and physical thrill of sports, competition, and hunting were essential aspects of life for many black slaves, yet recreational activities extended far beyond the limits of visceral activity and physical athleticism. These behaviors did not necessarily signify survival or even physical ventures for the slaves, but they provided the cultural foundations of slave communities. Researchers on slave culture reveal that such themes as music, dancing, weddings, and sports were all important aspects of the individual traditions within slave communities. The only social experiences many slaves ever encountered was the work they were forced to do every day.

The roots of traditional African sports included things like wrestling, jumping, running, ball games, and stick or spear throwing, all of which continued their cultural role as slaves from Africa adapted to a life of bondage in America. Wrestling was a prominent sport among Africans because their lives promoted themes of physicality and nature. The sport of wrestling represented a way of life for Africans. Another community recreational or sporting event among them was cornshucking, this event was considered to be a common social gathering on the southern plantation for the American slave. Cornshucking events were usually held on Saturday evenings. During cornshucking events people would play the fiddle and create music which allowed slaves of all ages and sexes to dance and enjoy themselves with one another, allowing them the opportunity to mentally liberate themselves from their daily pains and struggles. Music coupled with the cornshucking activities provided the slaves with a sense of enjoyment and independence.

Even when working in the fields, slaves would often sing as they slaved long hard days full of intense labor to fulfill their owners' daily demands. Many slaves learned to play instruments; they created their own music and interacted with fellow slaves when permitted. This allowed slaves a rare opportunity to experience individualism and intimacy as they would often engage in dancing, drinking, and recreation. On many plantations, slaves could only marry with the permission of the plantation owners, which led to formal customs and forms of celebration to create a cultural foundation for the American slave. They enjoyed events such as wedding ceremonies, dances, and parties during these brief holidays. This would typically be done by the man and woman holding hands and jumping over a broom, a tradition equal to modern customs of crossing the threshold into the family's new home.

Running was another noteworthy sport for slaves and is still popular today among blacks. Running has always been a prominent physical aspect of life in Africa and America. Before slavery, the men in tribes would tend to livestock in pastures far from their homes and would often have run back and forth to the location of their daily slave chores. The younger boys would engage in races against their peers, highlighting their speed and quickness in the various individual athletic competitions. Jumping was another essential sport in African culture, particularly to young boys transitioning to manhood. The ability to leap great heights or lengths proved a man's strength and physical capabilities. Physical status was an attribute respected by many tribal African communities. Hence, jumping symbolized the ability to overcome the natural surroundings, creating a value for this particular activity within the communities.

During slavery, baseball, boxing, running, wrestling, and horseracing were competitive sports that became popular in America during the eighteenth and nineteenth centuries. The sport of horseracing dates back to before the establishment of the American colonies in the seventeenth century. Baseball also helped to transform America during this time. With the introduction of town ball in the Massachusetts area, the sport began to take shape in American society in the eighteenth century. Wrestling dates back to an even earlier period in history. As numerous sports bridge the gap between African and American culture when it comes to American slavery, all of these types of recreational involvement show a distinct relationship with the recreational culture of the American slave.

Town ball, wrestling, and boxing not only found popularity among African and African-American slaves, but also in the sports realm of white America. The advancement of these sports would become a social craze. Both white Americans and black slaves participated in the game of town ball providing a common experience despite the social distinctions between the two groups. This sport for both free white Americans and African Americans in bondage became an essential piece of recreational enjoyment. Town ball was one of the few sports that gave both adults and children, of either race, a chance to enjoy physical activity and competition. Like many of the other sports allowed to American slaves, games went on after work was finished, especially on holidays and time off. On the plantation, town ball quickly became one of the most popular sports among slaves. This was due to its minimal physical danger and the ability for a large group of slaves to participate in the activity.

Running dates back to the preslavery era and was always a sport of convenience and enjoyment in African culture. American culture found running to be popular amongst both the areas earliest inhabitants and whites during the colonial and modern eras. Native African tribes utilized the open plain landscapes and areas of their homelands to engage in this sport. The tradition of running as a recreational amusement was continuously passed on and became a practical sport for American slaves in the southern United States. During cornshucking festivals, holiday events, and even at night in the cornfields or backlands, many slaves enjoyed the thrill of racing against one another. Running was not the easiest sport for slave participants. Slaves rarely had shoes or covering for their feet, making this a painful venture.

Long before slavery, Africans had established a tradition incorporating running. Later, slaves sometimes embarked on recreational races for personal satisfaction. It is equally important to note that this was a pre-modern-day entertainment for the white salve owners. Many of the sports that slaves enjoyed had elements of great danger involved. In fact, women and some slave children were unable to physically partake in some of the more strenuous recreational events that took place on the plantation.

Children did enjoy dancing, music, cornshucking, and most of all, marbles, a game of no danger and of little consequence to the slave masters. Children used the game of marbles as the primary form of recreational escape. This game was still a childhood pastime during the 1970s in America. White children also played this particular game. Unusually in the realm of recreational pursuits, slaves and white children were allowed to both play and compete with one another during their early years. The rules of this game required a circle approximately ten feet in diameter drawn on the ground. The primary objective was to knock the opponent's marble out of the ring. Slave children would draw a circle in the dirt, either in the slave cabins, which were predominantly built on dirt lots using the earth as the floor, or outside in nearby areas, and would use homemade marbles to play. Marbles are made out of rocks and stones. These marbles were the essential pieces used by slave children to play this game.

Horse racing was one of the most elaborate and exhilarating sporting events for American slaves. Horses were easily accessible on the plantation as they were used daily on southern farms, though they were often kept away from the slaves, it was not impossible to sneak the animals away. Horse racing was a far more dangerous event primarily enjoyed by adult males, but simply riding horses was something that slaves of all ages and genders enjoyed on the plantation. Slave children also rode horses as an enjoyable recreational sport. Horse races were rarely communal events, as most participants were the men who had primary access to the animals. Because slaves had a difficult time getting horses away from the main plantation, slaves mixed recreational horseracing and riding with the daily grind of the plantation work.

These sports, like many of the others, found slaves competing against one another for bragging rights and for material items not easily obtained due to the constraints of American slavery. Horse racing in its more traditional form most often happened away from the work areas on the plantation. Slaves took horses into the open back fields near their residences and held secret events that pitted slave against slave in a fast-paced race atop a powerful horse. Sports played during slavery time meant much more to slaves than just a form of recreation or an active involvement in communal regards. Slaves played an abundance of games and coexisted with other slaves who also may have been stripped of the same basic human rights at the hands of their white owners. American slaves were willing to risk their lives and freedom to enjoy late-night horseraces and other events as well.

Many slave owners and plantations overseers placed more value on the farm animals than they did on the human slave workers. It was through such sporting or recreational events that American slaves were able to feel a sense of worth beyond their normal comparison to the animals maintained throughout the South.

Those early sports heroes in shackles may have experienced extremely complex psychological and emotional distress. Slaves dealt with the unimaginable horrors of American slavery in the South. They used recreational habits and sports to create a social and cultural world that allowed them to be human, if only for the moment. The cultural developments and sport habits found on southern plantations suggest that slaves were able to create some type of mental balance within the context of life for themselves, one filled with tradition, enjoyment, freedom, and culture. The American slave's desire for the development of culture and identity through sports ultimately was an attempt by the enslaved community to experience the basic principles of human existence, human freedom, and the pursuit of happiness during such horrific times in their life. Sporting events were and continue to be symbolic for both whites and blacks.

The Scholarships

During the 1960s, there was an increase in the number of young black athletes being recruited to major universities on athletic scholarships to participate in football, basketball, baseball, track and field and volleyball. For the most part prior to the 1960s the black athlete was restricted by universities' unwillingness to integrate. By the 1970s the professional ranks had also increased as a result of the new pipeline for the black athlete to do what they do best in their athletic ways. It is important to note that the Civil Rights Movement opened the doors for black athletes to enroll and play sports at elite white universities through athletic scholarships. Many black boys and girls are given athletic scholarships each year to play sports.

According to NPR commentator Frank Deford, sports play a significant role in the choices and, eventually, the adult lives of far too many black boys. Blacks are so obviously successful in athletics, while in general black males are not adequately noticeable in such areas of life as medicine, law, and even education. There seems to be a disproportionate number of black boys interested in sports especially basketball and football. Black boys, more so than black females are more than willing

11

to participate in sports and dedicate and commit their bodies in athletic activities rather than academic matter in the classroom. Many coaches have helped to fuel the countless sad stories of young black kids with only average athletic skills who are so eager and willing to give up serious preparation for life in the wasted pursuit of the fantasy of being the next LeBron James or Dwyane Wade.

For the black athlete hoping to play intercollegiate athletics, a college athletic scholarship is obviously a prize for very few black athletes. Within the black community a college athletic scholarship can serve as a lure for countless young blacks who see sports as their ticket out of a bad situation. The University of Pennsylvania conducted a study that revealed 64% of basketball players and 57% of football players in the six powerhouse American college conferences were black. However, blacks represent less than 3% of the student body at many of these same institutions, with the exception of sporting teams like track and field, basketball and football. Unfortunately, many black athletes are blatantly exploited by our colleges. Football and basketball are the true revenue-generating sports that continue to pay the majority of the bills for entire athletic departments, as well as putting money into the institutions' general funds. Many black athletes obviously need help, based upon social economic status and limited educational and social development. Nevertheless, they can help generate millions by running fast, jumping high, and playing like warriors on the football fields on Saturday afternoons, hoping to play in the NFL.

On the other hand, institutional rules strictly forbid student-athletes from benefiting personally or sharing in the revenue they help generate at the institutional level. However, the money made by the football and basketball teams fund the athletic scholarships and the salaries of coaches in other sports. This is not at all totally bad, given the fact that their efforts will help offer additional scholarships to athletes of color and hire coaches of color. Earning a college scholarship involves countless hours of arduous practice resulting in both physical sweat and emotional tears.

Millions of fans equate to billions of dollars, yet the athlete receives no compensation outside of their scholarships and the chance to play big-time sports at large universities. Not since the days of the plantations have those who perform such noteworthy assignments earned so very little. Similarly to the slaves who worked on the plantations, intercollegiate athletes engage in sweaty and dirty athletic competition on the fields, while the institutional overseers garner revenue from their labor.

Take a moment and consider the economic power of March Madness. During the 2014 basketball tournament, March Madness generated nearly $200 million for the NCAA and its membership. The NCAA total revenues and receipts for 2014 reached close to $1 billion. These revenues are largely based on television and media contacts. Each year, the NCAA disseminates about $188 million directly to its member conferences. The Atlantic Coast Conference (ACC) received $17.68 million for the 2011–2012 NCAA basketball tournament alone. The big five conferences earn the majority of the NCAA dollars (ACC, SEC, Pac 12, Big Ten, and Big 12). The argument was made that from the $140 million, the twenty-five dollars per game allotted to each player was compared to a slave's wage.

College football is no better than basketball. The Rose Bowl paid out $30 million in 2005, the median football coach's salary in Division I-A is $855,000 today. Among major conferences such as the ACC, Big East, Big Ten, Big 12, PAC-10, and SEC, the average football coach's salary is $1.4 million. On average, college football attracts over forty million fans to the games with annual revenues of $5 billion. Many of these institutions have world-class training facilities and stadiums with the best artificial turf, equipment, and skyboxes that TV money can buy to attract the most talented and gifted black athletes to help sell tickets and generate other revenue. Intercollegiate athletes are classified under student athletics. However, at the Division I level the graduation rate is 51% among football players and a meager 43% among basketball players. It is unfortunate that most black athletes at major universities are majoring in less than challenging coursework so they can focus much of their attention on their athletic labor on the fields and basketball courts. They practice and train just like big-league slave athletes, more concerned about the overseer, scoreboards, and less concerned with becoming educated. The real deal is that many of these institutions are recruiting young black men and women to play, in much the same way that big-league plantation owners went about selecting blacks for labor. Whether or not intercollegiate athletes should be paid their fair share of the multibillion-dollar pie will continue to be debated. Since the NCAA and large PWIs have decided to move forward with the pay for play rule, many student athletes of color are now receiving upwards of $10,000 to $12,000 dollars per semester which is based largely on the value of their scholarship and their social economic status. Furthermore, many of these student athletes are receiving little if any financial literacy education from these institutions. My recommendation is that a percentage of the scholarship values for student-athletes, should be placed into a trust fund that could only be dispensed once student-athlete college careers have ended or they graduate with a college degree. This would provide a head start in life for the student-athlete. If the student-athlete decides to forgo college for the professional ranks, they will no longer be eligible. Furthermore, colleges and universities must do a better job helping former athletes return to school tuition free following their playing careers so that they can get a degree.

CHAPTER TWO

A Conversation with Three Sports Angels

"To cheapen the lives of any group of men, cheapens the lives of all men, even our own. This is a law of human psychology, or human nature. And it will not be repealed by our wishes, nor will it be merciful to our blindness."

—William Pickens

Little did I know that when my family and I decided to attend church services at Saint Michael and All Angels Episcopal Church for the very first time, that the greeter at the front of the church as was a basketball pioneer from days gone. The greeter was a tall black gentleman who looked like he might have played basketball back in the day. He was Jackie Moore, a classy old dude who was overly welcoming and nice. You would have never known that Jackie Moore was a trailblazer for so many young black basketball players; he opened the doors for so many blacks. Despite being the first black collegiate athlete to play basketball at LaSalle University and in the NBA with the Philadelphia Warriors, John "Jackie" Moore is now retired and lives in Charlotte, North Carolina, at the tender age of eighty-four. He is a passionate NBA fan who is a regular at Charlotte Hornet games. According to Moore, he never really saw himself as a hero or a pioneer. Playing basketball was just something Moore really enjoyed in the 1940s. During the late forties and early fifties, few blacks were playing basketball in the Philadelphia community where he grew up. While at LaSalle and with the NBA Warriors, most of the time Moore was the only black player on the court. Moore lived on the west side of Philadelphia, not necessary its best side. Moore lived and grew up in a mixed neighborhood. In fact, the high school that Moore attended was largely Jewish.

In the fall of 1951, Moore became the first black athlete to play for La Salle University. From 1951 to 1954, Moore played for the La Salle Explorers. After college, Moore played with the Philadelphia Warriors. The La Salle University Athletic Department inducted Jackie Moore into the Athletic Hall of Fame on February 1, 2014. While at La Salle, Moore helped lead the Explorers to the 1952 NIT Championship. For those who may not know, the NIT was the current version of the NCAA March Madness we love today. After leaving La Salle, Moore went on to play three seasons in the National Basketball Association and he also won a NBA World Championship with the Philadelphia Warriors in 1956.

While reflecting on his days at La Salle, Moore indicated that he rarely played against other black players in college because he was always the only black player on the court most of the time. According to Moore, it was the same way when he arrived in the pros. Moore indicated that few blacks were playing organized basketball during the mid-1940s. When he was not in school, Moore played a lot of basketball at the Haddington Recreation Center where other local Philly standouts played. According to Moore, there was an abundance of great ball players in his neighborhood, but, for various reasons, many of them did not play high school basketball. He grew up playing on the same courts that produced storybook basketball stars such as Wilt Chamberlain, Wall James, Walt Hazzard, Wayne Hightower, and Lewis Lloyd. It was Moore who established the foundation and path for great Philly players to follow. During the late 1940s and 1950s, Moore was considered to be the top high school player in Philly. According to Moore, there were other good black players in Philly, but they were not afforded the opportunity to play for any of the white institutions, such as LaSalle University, that embraced segregation. The other black players who wanted to go to college all attended HBCUs in the south. During his first season at LaSalle, Moore helped the team earn the NIT Championship. Moore describes his time at LaSalle as a mixture of joy and pain. The joy was that he was able to play the game he so loved, but the pain came from his rough encounters with opposite teams while on the road; they had yet to include blacks on their teams. There was also pain in terms of the travel accommodations; they were very challenging to say the least. Many hotels and restaurants refused to serve blacks. To their credit, the LaSalle team was united as one and refused to tolerate any form of racial discrimination.

LaSalle was the largest and only white institution to offer Moore a basketball scholarship. Life was fine for Moore when he enrolled at LaSalle in the late 1940s. He enjoyed a great relationship with his teammates and his coaches. The main problem for Moore occurred only when the game started. His teammates and coaches did whatever they could to support him and encourage him on all fronts. They even agreed as a team to cancel or not play some games because of how Moore would be treated. Moore was often denied the right to eat at many restaurants and hotels where LaSalle played. By some standards Moore has been regarded as the second-best player to come out of city of brotherly love behind Wilt Chamberlain. Moore was a 6' 5", 192-lb power forward star at Philadelphia's legendary Overbrook High School, the same high school that produced Wilt Chamberlain. Prior to enrolling at La Salle, Moore was one of the top basketball players in Philly. He stated that he was very fortunate to play for La Salle because the local colleges weren't recruiting black players. Moore said he never really thought seriously about being the first black to play at La Salle. Within the athletic community at La Salle, life was not overly difficult Moore recalls.

From his days at La Salle, Moore recounted some rough times on the road with his teammates. The team's travel accommodations had to be changed because some restaurants would not serve blacks. Moore stated that the team tolerated no racial discrimination. The team always operated as a team. He recounts that the team always ate dinner together, and if we were told that blacks could not be served, then the team would not eat there. Moore said that it was not easy, but he dealt with it as well as he could.

Moore's accounts from playing in the NBA indicated that it was much harder for the few black players. Blacks had to be extraordinarily talented to play in the NBA. There was a limit on the number of black players in the league, you had to be a great player, not a good player, if you were just as good as a white player, but the white would end up making the team. After a solid career at LaSalle, Moore moved up the ranks of the NBA, where things proved to be much tougher not just with the talent and skill level, but the level of racism. There were only a few (three to four) blacks players in the NBA when Moore arrived and only a handful when he departed in the mid-1950s. According to Moore, during this era of the NBA, a black man had to be a sensational athletic talent to play professional basketball in a league of nearly all white men. All of the teams were owned by Jews. Most teams were only owned by one person; there were not partner or joint owners. Teams had a limit on the number of black players who could join a team during the NBA's segregation era.

Moore only earned about $12,000 per season as a pro. The highest paid player during his era was Bob Cousy, who earned about $25,000. There were no super shoe contacts or endorsement deals or pensions. Today, Moore has been included to the NBA's pension program, thanks largely to the NBA players association of which he is a member.

Despite not playing a lengthy professional career in the NBA—he only played with the Philadelphia Warriors from 1955 to 1956—he did capture an NBA Championship ring. When Moore first joined the Warriors, he was reunited with former college teammates from LaSalle, Paul Arzon, Neil Johnson, George Dempsey, Ernie Beck, and Tom Gola. After leaving the Warriors, Moore joined the Boston Celtics for a short time before suffering a career-ending injury. Moore is a big part of black history in the NBA. His name is frequently mentioned with Earl Lloyd, Chuck Cooper, Harold Hunter, and Nat "Sweetwater" Clifton as the first real black starting five in the NBA. Earl Lloyd was the first black to play in an NBA game. He played for the Washington Capitals during 1950–1951; Jackie Moore and Earl Lloyd did a great deal to help change things for the future game of basketball that so many enjoy today. They were instrumental in helping to establish the ground rules for the likes of Wilt Chamberlain and others.

Every time he entered the court, Moore experienced prejudiced actions by the opposing white teams and their fans. They were completely against blacks integrating college sports. Moore recounts having to play the game he so loved very carefully and wisely at all times to avoid getting hurt. Moore was the subject of countless intended rough fouls and sanctioned physical roughhouse play by the white players. This type of play often resulted in stitches and even the loss of several teeth at the hands of overly aggressive white players who wanted to make a statement to Moore and other black players that they were really not wanted.

I was granted the wonderful opportunity to sit down with Moore while working to complete this book to pick his brain about his experiences associated with sports. The conversation with Jackie Moore went like this.

Charles Pinckney: So, Moore, tell me your thoughts about why you attended LaSalle during the time that you attended and what did it really mean to you, a young black student-athlete during the time you integrated college sports at LaSalle?

Jackie Moore: What I really liked about LaSalle was that it was close to home and family members. It was an up-and-coming college and there were not a lot of people talking about LaSalle. To be the first black to suit up for LaSalle and play meant a lot for me and the black community in Philly who followed my career. I was looked up to by so many younger black players in the community. I was somewhat of a role model or example for younger players in Philly.

Charles Pinckney: Now you are a former college athlete and a basketball pioneer. So how did you make sense of racism in sports?

Jackie Moore: As in many cities and neighborhoods, racism was very prevalent. Therefore, many white players did not want to play with blacks or against blacks. Usually blacks had to be much better than white players. Often times a black player and white player usually had similar skills. After integration took place and when white and black players were on the court, the white players always got the call in their favor. The refs would allow white players to do get away with murder. It was very common to be called negative names from the fans, and even the white players from the opposing teams.

Charles Pinckney: Okay, so what does it mean to be a black conscious athlete during your playing days both in college and the NBA?

Jackie Moore: If you are speaking of the ills of society, those who were under privileged with a feeling of hopelessness and a lack of purpose for living, being black meant not having the opportunity to advance economically or socially. Many of those things I was not aware of, so I did not speak about them. I became more aware of the ills of society after my playing days had ended.

Charles Pinckney: Tell me how important is the black athlete's social environment?

Jackie Moore: All black athletes are in need of a good social environment. There are many pitfalls in society such as alcohol, drugs, and even sex and prostitution. There always seems to be some type of relationship between athletes and drug dealers. In many cases, the dealers are always attempting to lure athletes to their world either as users or close associates. In terms of women and sex, it has always been the weakness of far too many black athletes both past and present. There is the issue of pregnancy, multiple out-of-marriage children and child support or lack of child support. It is important that today's athlete become more aware of the many pitfalls and surround themselves with more positive people. It is also important that they think about what is best for them in both the short term and the long term. They need to make better decisions and realize that so many people are looking up to them as role models or heroes.

Charles Pinckney: During your days at LaSalle, you state that your team operated as one when you faced discrimination. Was this effort to combat racism forced upon the team by the coaching staff and administration, or was it a voluntary effort by teammates? Were there any team members who were unwilling to take a stand in your defense?

Jackie Moore: The entire team was from the Philadelphia area. In fact, I played against most of them in high school and on the local playground in the city. For the most part, we were all somewhat well acquainted and there was a level of mutual respect. Everyone on the team, including the coaches always made a strong and honest commitment to combat discrimination on my behalf. Despite playing college basketball at a majority-white college and being the only black player on the team, we all really bonded and became lifelong friends.

Charles Pinckney: As a black ball player competing against whites, were you ever intimidated while playing the game? Did you ever question your belonging when it came to skills and ability to play the game due to the lack of black recruits, or were you aware that blacks were being overlooked simply due to their skin color?

Jackie Moore: I was never intimidated by anyone, nor did I intimidate anyone. I was just there to play the game. I was just a black kid from Philadelphia who could run, jump, and shoot well. I did have a level of playground toughness. My height and my ball handling skills were somewhat superior to a lot of the white players who I opposed. I always worked hard to improve my game because I knew I had to always be at the top of my game. During the fifties, growing up in the city of brotherly love (Philadelphia), I was not really aware that blacks athletes were often overlooked by many white colleges simply because of the color of their skin or race. But, LaSalle recruited me despite the color of my skin and race.

Charles Pinckney: When you did play against black players, did you feel a sense of unity despite being on opposing teams? If so, were you as competitive with them as you were with whites?

Jackie Moore: No, I did not feel in any way a sense of unity when I played against other teams that had black players. The main goal was always winning the game, no matter who you were playing against. I always played hard, against any and every one all of the time.

Charles Pinckney: Looking back on your collegiate experience, are you satisfied with your decision to attend a historically white university or do you wish you attended a HBCU?

Jackie Moore: I would have to say that I was very satisfied to attend a historically white university. In the fifties, there was very little recruiting of black athletes by any universities. So I felt very fortunate to be notice and even more honored to be selected by the coaches at LaSalle to join the all-white basketball team and contribute right away. The only other colleges that recruited me were two historically black colleges (Maryland State and Saint Augustine's in Raleigh, NC).

Charles Pinckney: What is your stance on the NBA's diversity today? For example, many argue that the greatest players to ever play the game are black, however the NBA's logo is a silhouette of a white player in Jerry West. West is considered a pioneer of the game, however the individual statistics and number of championships accumulated by West do not compare to the likes of Mike, Magic, Wilt, or Oscar. Do you feel that in a league that has been dominated by black athletes and influenced by black culture, a black player should be the logo?

Jackie Moore: I personally do not have any problem with the NBA logo "presumably" of Jerry West's silhouette. When the NBA logo was adopted, Jerry West was one of the most popular players in the NBA. For the most part, team compositions were primarily made up of white players, and there were very few black players. I do not think that the decision was based on championships or scoring titles, but more so on the player's actual image and persona.

Charles Pinckney: Thank you so much Mr. Jackie Moore, it was indeed my pleasure talking with you during the development of this book.

My next interview was with Jim Burch, one of the first black referees in a major basketball conference. It was an honor to read about his remarkable efforts and even more rewarding for me to talk personally with him about his drive to break ground for other blacks. In the late 1960s, Jim Burch became the first black men's basketball official in the Southern Conference and was among the first in the ACC. In his educational career, his hiring as the assistant state superintendent for administrative services in the North Carolina Department of Public Instruction in 1970 made national news. At that time, he was the highest ranking black in the North Carolina public schools. All of these accomplishments were unheard of for a black man in those times, and Burch is still going strong today. At age eighty-eight, he is the coordinator of officials for men's and women's basketball for the Central Intercollegiate Athletic Association (CIAA). Even today, Jim Burch is still making calls and breaking barriers.

Burch is a true pioneer in terms of men's basketball officials. Despite being close to ninety years old, he is still physically and actively involved in the game of basketball as conference coordinator. Burch's passion for officiating basketball runs deep, as he worked his first high school game in 1953 and was only paid $3 per game. Burch, who graduated from Fayetteville Teachers College (now Fayetteville State University), where he played football and baseball while earning a degree in elementary education, eventually became a collegiate official and began working games in the CIAA, a league where all the members are HBCUs. The year was 1967 that Burch, seeking to do more and become more integrated within the context of officiating basketball games, reached out in a letter to the coordinator of officials of the Southern Conference, J. Dallas Shirley, seeking to be allowed by the all-white conference that had no black officials to officiate basketball games.

At that point in his career Burch was already forty years old and was initially told by Shirley that he was too old to work as an official for the Southern Conference and that the age limit was thirty-five. After Burch claimed discrimination and challenged Shirley's decision, Burch was invited to attend an officiating meeting at Duke University in Durham, North Carolina. When Burch arrived on the campus at Duke University, some of the other white referees' were not at all happy to welcome Burch. In fact, two of the white referees were quick to question Burch's reason for being at the meeting. Burch remembers going to the meeting and when he sat down, two white officials asked him what he was doing there. Surprisingly, Shirley immediately supported Burch and told the other whites in attendance that Burch had just as much a right to be here as anyone else.

During Burch's remarkable career, he has been inducted into seven halls of fame and was an alternate official for the 1977 Men's Final Four. In 1969 after two short years of officiating freshman basketball games, Burch was voted by the coaches in the Southern Conference to work varsity basketball games. The same year, he was admitted in the ACC. Burch reported that during his early days of integrating basketball officiating, he encountered intense racial taunts and verbal abuse from white fans. Burch worked in the CIAA for twenty-nine years, the Southern Conference for twenty-one years and the ACC for eighteen years. He also worked games in the Mid-Eastern Athletic Conference and Sun Belt Conference and has refereed in eleven NCAA tournaments to date, the remarkable history of a true sports pioneer. As an athletic administrator and faculty member at one of the current CIAA institutions, I have been fortunate enough to be in the same room with Burch on a several occasions. The conversation with Burch went like this.

Charles Pinckney: So Mr. Burch tell me your thoughts about being the first black to officiate basketball in the Southern Conference and one of the first in the Atlantic Coast Conference?

Jim Burch: At the time, that was the least thing on my mind. I just wanted to referee, and I had the confidence to feel that I could do the job.

Charles Pinckney: So can you help me to make sense of racism in sports both past and present in terms of being a basketball official at the collegiate level?

Jim Burch: On the court, one is judged by his or her ability to do the job in a satisfactory manner. There were several incidents of racial slurs made towards me; a few that were very derogatory and mean spirited. That was expected. I had received similar racial comments in my daily life as a person and as an educator.

Charles Pinckney: What does it mean to be called a pioneer?

Jim Burch: I never really think about it until someone brings it to my attention. But to honestly answer your question—nothing. It is just something that we as people use to express what is considered to be first for our race. Again, I just wanted an equal opportunity to be involved in a specific facet of American life as we know it.

Charles Pinckney: Tell me your thoughts about why you chose to integrate the profession of refereeing?

Jim Burch: Again I never thought about it in that manner. It was something that I wanted to do and after watching others do it, I knew I could do as well as they did or better.

Charles Pinckney: What kind of progress have we made based on today's number of black referees?

Jim Burch: A tremendous amount of progress if progress is measured by participation. You hardly ever see a sport, high school, college, or professional, without there being at least one black official working a game.

Charles Pinckney: Can you please share your thoughts on the need to develop a pool of black officials?

Jim Burch: It is a must. We have to continue to develop others to take the place of the large number of black game officials that are working today's sports contests as they reach the retirement age.

Charles Pinckney: What kind of roadblocks did you have to overcome before you were allowed to officiate in the ACC?

Jim Burch: I had to first believe that I could do the job, and not let anyone tell me that I could not do it. I could not afford to get down on myself when I made an error on the court, and, finally, I had to want and believe that I could succeed.

Charles Pinckney: How were you treated by nonblack officials and white fans?

Jim Burch: In the beginning, at times a little rough by fans. I had very few problems with nonblack officials when they realized that I could referee. I got abuse from both black and white fans at times. That is the price that a basketball referee pays when he or she walks on the court. You see, a referee causes some individual's mind to react negatively just by the fact that you are a referee.

Charles Pinckney: What was the attitude of teams, coaches, and fans as you were the first black official in the South? Was there a lot of attention and support from the black community?

Jim Burch: A tremendous amount of support from the black community and the white community. My employer in the Charlotte-Mecklenburg County Schools and North Carolina Department of Public Instruction supported me 100%. They both thought that it was great that one of their own was on TV. As a side, when I made a call against their favorite team, I was reminded of it the next day when I returned to the workplace. The coaches were excellent, many were complimentary of my work. I was voted four times by coaches as the number-one official in the Southern Conference. I was treated as any other official by players. The usual complaining but nothing ever serious. You see I had the answer for any bad behavior by coaches and players—the vaunted T-Foul.

Charles Pinckney: You officiated in eleven NCAA tournament games eighteen years in the ACC and twenty-one with the Southern Conference. What are some of your most enriching memories?

Jim Burch: When I went to the Citadel in the late 1960s to start the game, they unfurled a large confederate flag from the ceiling and played their fight song, which was Dixie, prior to the singing of the national Anthem. I remember the radio announcer asking me how I felt when the Crop was singing Dixie. I remember telling him that I was there to referee a basketball game not to be involved in the Civil War, which had been over for more than a hundred years. Working the Pan American Games in Mexico City and in Puerto Rico was a great experience involving international teams. I was going to the Olympics in 1980, but President Carter canceled the American participation in the games in Russia. Lastly, working my first NCAA Division I tournament game, my first ACC tournament game. The greatest thrill was working a triple overtime championship game in the CIAA between North Carolina A&T and Norfolk State in which Norfolk State won 136–133 in the Greensboro Coliseum after working the North Carolina High School Athletic Conference 4-A Championship game the same afternoon prior to the CIAA Championship game that night.

Charles Pinckney: What advice would you offer the NCAA in an effort to encourage and secure more black men and women as officials?

Jim Burch: A concerted effort with a formal training program provided and paid for by the High School Athletic Association, the NCAA and the NBA. This to include camps, summer league play, AAU games and various other games to provide potential aspirants an opportunity to develop their officiating skills. A small honorarium could be paid to the participants also.

Charles Pinckney: What advice would you provide for student-athletes interested in officiating sporting events?

Jim Burch: You must really want to do it. In other words, you must love it. It cannot be done for the money in the beginning. But if you develop your skills and become very good, money can be made. You must believe in yourself. Self-confidence is the key to success in officiating.

Charles Pinckney: Obviously you have officiated tons of games during your career. Please share some of the basketball players that you have witnessed up close who were so amazing. Who were some of the greatest black basketball players that you had the opportunity to officiate during your outstanding career?

Jim Burch: Of all the players that I have refereed during my career Earl Monroe was the best college player and that includes Michael Jordan who became great as a professional. David Thompson and Ralph Sampson were also great college players. However, Earl Monroe was far ahead of his time in what he could do with a basketball.

Charles Pinckney: What advice would you offer to young black men and women today about the profession of officiating?

Jim Burch: Work hard at your craft. If you do not love it, get out of it; believe in your ability. Learn all of the nuisances about the game, never think that you have arrived or know it all. You can always learn. And live a clean life. In conclusion, it is ironic or an American tragedy that so many individuals in education or sports officiating before me had the ability, the mental toughness, the skills and qualifications but were denied an opportunity to exhibit the talents due to the color of their skin or their ethnicity.

The third and final angel that I have been blessed to be associated with is none other than my Episcopal brother in Christ, George Williams. I had the opportunity to work with Williams when I was first hired in the Psychology Department at Saint Augustine University. Williams and I also attended the same Episcopal church in Raleigh from 2001 to 2005. After leaving Saint Augustine University in the fall in 2005, our paths crossed again in Nashville, Tennessee, at the 2007 NCAA Convention. George Williams has built an empire in track and field and cross-country at Saint Augustine's University in Raleigh, North Carolina. He began coaching track and field in 1976, and he has won an amazing thirty-eight national championships as a coach.

The legendary Williams has over forty years as the principal architect of the Saint Augustine's University track and field program. He has won more championships than any current coach in his sport to date. Since becoming the head track-and-field coach at Saint Augustine's University, he has won an astonishing 108 conference championships between the men's and women's teams. In addition, he has also won a total of 38 national championships at the NCAA Division II level, which is truly amazing. Williams has coached thirty-two Olympians, including three gold medalists. He has also been the recipient of more than 100 track and field coach of the year honors, including the 2010 Division II national outdoor men's coach of the year, awarded by the U.S. Track & Field and Cross-Country Coaches Association. One of Williams' most treasured honors includes being selected as the Head Coach of the 2004 Men's Olympic Track and Field Team in Athens, Greece. In 1996, Williams served as assistant coach of the 1996 U.S. Olympic Track and Field Team in Atlanta, GA., where each athlete he was responsible for won a gold medal. In 1999, Williams was selected as the U.S. Men's head coach at the World Outdoor Championships in Seville, Spain. He also coached the Indoor Championships in Toronto, Canada, and the 1992 IAAF World Cup in Havana, Cuba. In addition to being the track and field and cross-country head coach, Williams is also the university's Athletic Director. Williams graduated from then Saint Augustine's College in 1965.

Prior to taking over the now framed track and field and cross-country program, he worked in a variety of roles including Director of Alumni Affairs, Admissions Counselor, Director of Student Activities, and Assistant Basketball Coach. In 1997 Williams was named athletic director. Under Williams' leadership as athletic director and track and field and cross-country head coach, his teams have collected over a 150 CIAA track and field and cross-country conference championships. Additionally, he boasts of graduating 95% of his student-athletes.

According to Williams, when he first began coaching track and field athletes, he knew very little. A close friend, legendary Winston-Salem basketball coach Clarence "Big House" Gaines told the young Williams after watching one of his track events that if he wanted to compete he needed to recruit track and field athletes, not basketball athletes. Williams was a star basketball player during his days at Saint Augustine's College.

According to many sources, Williams had a sweet jump shot and he could really score the ball. Williams was such an outstanding basketball player at Saint Augustine's College in the 1960s that he earned All CIAA honors and was offered a contract by the NBA's Detroit Pistons. Williams was highly influenced by Clarence "Big House" Gaines.

Apparently Williams was listening to what Big "House" Gaines told him about recruiting student-athletes that can run fast. According to Williams, there is no real secret to his team's abilities to winning in track and field. It is all about going out and recruiting the athletically gifted student-athletes who love running and wish to get a college education along the way. Williams states that he does not do a lot of changing with his coaching approach; it is all about biomechanics, because each student-athlete is different. Our athletes today have better tracks and lighter shoes. I was so honored to be associated with George as a former church member and to work with him on intercollegiate athletic business over the years. It was an even greater honor for me to talk with George and to be able to share his athletic experiences. The conversation with George Williams went like this.

Charles Pinckney: So, George, tell me your thoughts about what does it really mean to be a black athlete in the twenty-first century?

George Williams: There are more opportunities for black athletes than in the past, thanks in part to the integration of college and professional sports in the United States. Being a track and field coach, I must acknowledge the 1968 Olympics games in Mexico City, where John Carlos and Tommy Smith raised their black-gloved fists and bowed their heads solemnly while the U.S. national anthem was played during the medal ceremonies. I would have to believe that the united efforts of Carlos and Smith did help to increase the opportunities for the future of black athletes.

Charles Pinckney: Now you are a former college athlete and one of the winningest coaches in all three divisions of the NCAA, so how did you make sense of racism in sports?

George Williams: I do not focus on racism. I only focus on student-athletes that I have encountered to try to make them the best. Now, to be honest, racism does exist in sports. The majority of institutions, including track and field teams within the NCAA who are competing for championship, are employing in large parts young men and women of color. I am not saying that white kids cannot, but the numbers do not lie, black kids seem to run faster. Therefore, as a coach, you want that young man or woman who can run the fastest. It just so happens to be that race now becomes that common variable in the recruiting process.

Charles Pinckney: Okay, so what does it mean to be a black conscious athlete today?

George Williams: First of all being conscious of who you are. In the past, black athletes like Muhammad Ali, Jim Brown and Kareem Abdul-Jabbar had a strong understanding of their black consciousness and they were completely connected to the communities. Ali, Brown, and Jabbar had a tremendous amount of courage during very difficult times where blacks in general were more likely to remain silent on pressing issues. Now today, we have far more black athletes making tons of money, but only a very few have the courage to speak up on pressing issues that impact blacks. We must engage in a conservative effort of liberation and education for this new generation of black athletes, so that our future black athletes will understand the power that they possess at the collegiate and professional levels.

Charles Pinckney: Tell me how important is the black athlete's social environment?

George Williams: I think social settings and communities where black athletics live and play are very important because the majority of our black athletes derive from communities far below the United States poverty level. With that being said, it is important to note that psychologically, coaches have to work much harder to help the black athletes make the necessary adjustment from the past environment and communities to their new community which is often more diversified. This is not necessarily an easy task because you are talking about taking a kid out of an environment in which he or she has grown and developed a set of beliefs, values and attitudes for nearly eighteen years or more. So you see that in itself is a huge task for any coach. But we must do all we can to help the black athlete to change their thinking about their less-than-healthy social background in which they have been socialized.

Charles Pinckney: Why do you choose to remain at St. Augustine University, despite your numerous accomplishments? Have you been offered other positions at schools in power conferences and better funding? If so, what keeps you so loyal to the HBCU?

George Williams: I choose to remain at St. Augustine's University in order to give back to the university, and I feel it is the best place to help our black students. It was St. Augustine's College that made the investment in me by affording me the opportunity to become a student-athlete many moons ago. Yes, you are very correct; I could have left St. Augustine's University many times over to coach at a number of larger institutions with all of the resources you could imagine, but St. Augustine's is where it all started for me. I am in love with this institution, my past and present student-athletes and the athletic staff here are St. Augustine's University.

Charles Pinckney: Do you feel obligated to recruit black athletes as oppose to white? Do you see color when you recruit? For example, you have a black kid who comes from a rough area and has had a tough upbringing, and on the other hand you have a white kid who lived a very sheltered life. Both are equally athletic, possess similar skill sets, and are good students. Which one gets the last scholarship offer and why?

George Williams: I look at passion and commitment of the student-athlete not race. Reflecting back to one of your earlier questions; it just so happens that when it comes to track and field, at the end of the day, you are more likely to identify black athletes who participate in track and field. Now please note this, that if I can lure a nonblack track and field athletes who can help win championships, I and the university will welcome them with open arms.

Charles Pinckney: Track is dominated by black athletes but how is the diversity amongst coaches? Are black coaches given the same opportunity as whites at major institutions?

George Williams: No, they are not given the same opportunity. It is true that black coaches face enormous obstacles in obtaining positions in the coaching on all levels. It is unfortunate that these obstacles continue to exist despite the number of black athletes who graduate colleges and universities who are seeking coaching opportunities. In short, there is little correlation between the excellence of athletic abilities and their upward mobility similarly to white athletes who desire to coach after their playing days have ended.

Charles Pinckney: How have you been so successful when it comes to the graduation rates of your athletes? What have you done specifically to prepare your athletes for life after track and how have you been able to emphasize the importance of education?

George Williams: Education is a part of my recruiting tools. When I recruit an athlete for my team, there are three important things that we always tell all of our athletes. First they are told that "Academic" is priority number one. Track and Field comes second and that their controlled social behavior is third. I try to instill that into them daily before our work out and if they cannot abide by any of the three that they cannot be associated with the St. Augustine's University athletic department.

CHAPTER THREE

Is There a Future for the Black-Athlete in Intercollegiate Athletics

"I think over the next thirty years we are going to continue to see a decline of black athletic participation. The overwhelming majority of black athletes come out of the lower echelons of black society. I don't think it is accidental when you look at the inordinate number of blacks in jail and the proportionate number of blacks not on athletic teams. You are essentially looking at the same guy. They both have numbers; they are both in uniforms, and they both belong to gangs. They only call one the Crips, or the Bloods, while they call the other team the 49ers, Warriors, As, or the Giants. They are all in pursuit of respect. They all, at one level or another, keep score. The parallels are all there. It is the same guy. But I think what you are looking at over the next thirty years is that the guy in the jail uniform is going to outstrip, in both numbers and impact, the guy in the athletic uniform. I think the next thirty years is going to see that kind of transformation. We are going to be looking at the same guy, but only increasingly he is going to be wearing a jailhouse number, a jailhouse uniform, instead of a sports team number, and an athletic uniform."

—Harry Edwards

Is the future of intercollegiate athletics really at stake on the backs of the black athlete? Prior to the 1960s, very few black athletes had the opportunity to play football or basketball at predominately white institutions. In terms of sports, these institutions were everything except black. Between the 1960s and well into the 1970s, the college experiences for the black athlete at predominately white institutions were much more challenging than many can imagine. The social adjustment, expectation, and academic culture were all huge. At a number of predominately white institutions, socially minded faculty members were interested in the racial movement that was sweeping the nation. They were very vocal in forcing policy changes that increased the number of black student-athletes on campus.

As the first few black athletes were moving onto various institutions of higher education, they were also facing high levels of racial turmoil due to the color of their skin. On the heels of passing of the Civil Rights Bill, doors were opened for the black athlete to enroll and participate in intercollegiate athletics at predominantly white institutions. The history of racism in the South has been and, by some accounts, today is still well documented. Suddenly, black athletes during the 1960s were enrolling and playing football or basketball at elite white institutions. Predominately white institutions such as the University of Wyoming, University of Washington, Buffalo State, Oregon State University, Syracuse University, and the University of California at Berkeley all knew the benefits of inclusion.

It is equally important to note that very few black athletes had played prior to the influx of blacks during the 1960s. The most notable players were Paul Robeson at Rutgers University in 1910 and Ernest "Ernie" Davis, the first black athlete at Syracuse University from 1959 to 1961. The great migration of black athletes during 1960s to predominantly white institutions was a full-court press against racism and discrimination in our nation's most prestigious institutions. From the 1960s to the early 1970s, a number of black student-athletes decided to make their voices heard. During this time, a small number of black student-athletes, who were a part of several predominately white institutions' fiber, began to lead revolts, boycotts, and sit-ins to bring about some change in how black student-athletes was being treated.

This was a time of critical adjustment for both blacks and nonblacks at predominately white institutions and the outside communities that were home to these predominately white institutions. To say the least, these predominately white institutions were progressive in recruiting black student-athletes, but they were less progressive in addressing the issues of integration. There was no real plan to address the cultural difference and cultural sensitivity of the black student-athlete. There were no plans in place to hire black faculty, coaches, or administrators to match the black student-athlete. For the most part, black student-athletes had no one other than a few other black students to turn to. If they complained to their coaches, they were labeled as troublemakers and were often punished by their colleges. To say that there was a serious adjustment period for both the black and nonblack student-athletes would be an understatement. In most cases, it was safe to assume that both races were not altogether happy about their new teammates. By the late 1960s, many black student-athletes had reached a boiling point in terms of what they were willing to take. Several black student-athletes began speaking out about their conditions and how they were being treated by the predominately white institutions.

Black athletes consistently complained that they faced random acts of discrimination from members of the institutions, particularly the athletic department that had recruited them. It was not uncommon for the black athletes to endure derogatory comments about the color of their skin or their personal appearance. Furthermore, black-athletes were given poor living conditions compared to the white student-athletes. They were often grouped together and treated unfairly by the athletic training staff. In fact, their injuries were often not taken seriously by members of the athletic department. Black athletes also often reported that they would receive inferior academic advice. They were not taken seriously as students; for the most part they were only considered on campus to play sports and not to get an education. Most importantly, there were no black coaches or black athletic administrators that they could consult on matters of their ethnicity.

The continued complaints that black athletes voiced did nothing but further increase the tension among black and white athletes and the white-controlled institutions. These institutions knew that to keep the few blacks they had recruited, and if they were going to recruit blacks in the future, they must attempt to do better by all black athletes and the black student population in general. However, their immediate concerns were to make good on the promise to their prized black athletes by improving social conditions. This includes providing adequate campus housing, equal academic support, black coaches, and more sensitivity to the black athletes' emotional and medical concerns. Predominately white institutions acted, for the most part, on the heels of the civil rights bill, which many regarded as the most significant legislation ever passed. If majority universities were truly serious about recruiting and maintaining black athletes, they had to commit to improving the overall racial conditions for black athletes, which ultimately resulted in improved human rights for black athletes at predominantly white institutions. For most black athletes at predominantly white institutions during the 1960s, the issue of double standards for discipline and related matters continued to be a hot-button topic. Black athletes felt that white athletes were always given preferential treatment, while black athletes were always placed under a larger lens. Their every movement was being watched and monitored. If they acted out or violated any team rules they were often dealt with immediately and in some cases harshly; often, this resulted in removal from the team and revoking of athletic scholarships. Institutional racism at white institutions was a common practice during the 1960s despite the passing off the civil rights bill. There was a culture of institutional racism within predominantly white institutions and among athletic-department officials because they could get away with it.

In some regards, the conditions under which black student-athletes labored were tantamount to slavery on the plantation. This time the slave masters just happened to be white coaches with a whistle or cow bell. The main goal of recruiting black student-athletes was to establish a winning tradition, thus increasing revenue for predominately white institutions on the backs of a few black student-athletes. Predominately white institutions quickly found themselves searching for black student-athletes to run track and play basketball or football, two of the most popular sports then and now on the predominately white campus. Many black athletes withdrew from school and attended smaller predominantly white institutions, while others transferred to HBCUs in the south with less than adequate resources due to racial tensions. We will touch on the HBCUs and their struggles in a later chapter. In some cases the black-athlete's decision to transfer or leave the predominantly white institution was their choice, but in most cases it resulted in losing their scholarship for failing to comply with a set of athletic-department rules that were often later judged unfairly based on race.

As a result of the conditions that many black student-athletes were experiencing from their coaches and athletic departments, sports historian Dr. Harry Edwards reported that at least thirty-seven different revolts were led by black student-athletes on predominately white institution's campuses in 1968. According to Edwards, these revolts prompted predominately white institutions' presidents to revisit their commitment and take a more progressive stance to better meet the needs of black student-athletes. It was clear that predominately white institutions' presidents knew the potential dangers of recruiting black student-athletes and not being culturally sensitive to their educational and social needs. Predominately white institution presidents knew that if they were going to continue their efforts of recruiting more black students and black student-athletes, they had to fix the problem or at least clear up some of the major issues that the black student-athletes were protesting. Not only were black student-athletes speaking out, but they were also refusing to attend practices and to participate in games. Things had gone bad really quickly for many predominately white institutions for not doing right by their cash cow black student-athletes. For the most part, presidents at predominately white institutions understood that the real future of college sports was in jeopardy if the needs of the black student-athletes were not met.

Some of the demands of the black student-athletes included hiring black coaches and athletic trainers. One of the concerns lodged by black student-athletes was that trainers refused to treat their athletic injuries in the same manner as they treated nonblack athletes. They also wanted to see the creation of a black studies curriculum for future black student-athletes and other black students in general.

Black student-athletes also felt that they were issued a bad check. They believed that predominately white institutions had defaulted on their obligation by not ensuring that their basic of needs were met. The racial epithets and blatant acts of discrimination were more prevalent then and even today in sports at predominately white institutions. Many of the black student-athletes felt that coaches refused to provide them with a fair opportunity to earn a starting position because of the color of their skin. Before the storm would completely subside, a number of well-established coaches and athletic directors who refused to make the necessary changes to include black student-athletes in the predominately white institutions' communities were fired. The revolts, which included sit-ins and boycotts by black student-athletes, resulted from their being treated as less than human. It was common for some nonblack coaches to treat black student-athletes like animals and talk to them in the presence of other nonblacks like dirt. It was not uncommon for the white coaches and other athletic personnel to treat black student-athletes as the slave master treated slaves. Many black student-athletes were often humiliated by coaches based on how they dressed, talked, and socialized. Many black student-athletes felt that they were not welcome at predominately white institutions because of the color of their skin, which made life even more challenging. The black student-athletes' actions often resulted in less playing time and, in some cases, lost scholarships. These revolts also resulted in poor relationships between black and white athletes and occasional violence. Three major predominately white institutions with a strong social movement and desire during the 1960s to bring black student-athletes on campus included the University of California, Syracuse University, and Oregon State University. Some of the major grievances and concerns that eventually sparked revolts at predominately white institutions among black student-athletes between 1968 and 1972 are relevant today.

The many acts of racial discrimination and inadequate resources for all black student-athletes at predominately white institutions and HBCUs were major concerns. The birth of the black athlete's human rights movement can be traced back to the late 1960s when a few black athletes at predominantly white institutions one day said, enough is enough, we deserve to be treated better." Either you are going to treat us as human beings, or we are not to be a part of your athletic programs. Many black athletes were more than willing to forgo their athletic opportunities and educational experiences because of the high levels of inhumane treatment at the hands of white lead athletic departments that resembled Jim Crow attitudes and beliefs. The efforts of Martin Luther King, Jr. proved to be the catalyst for the black student-athletes during the 1960s. For the most part, the majority of their actions were nonviolent similar to MLK's to establish change for the betterment of the overall conditions of black student-athletes. Predominantly white institutions in general had no idea how to deal with the black student-athletes. The main goal at predominantly white institutions was to admit them and work things out over time. In other words, there was no real strategic plan in place to treat and value the black student-athlete as whole human citizens.

Grambling State University Boycott in 2013

Several members of the Grambling State University football team decided that enough was truly enough. Grambling State University (GSU) is a public HBCU located in the rural Grambling, Louisiana. Grambling State University is the home of late head football coach Eddie Robinson. Grambling State University has claimed fourteen black college football national championships and has a long-standing and rich legacy in sports. Grambling State University has produced more black professional athletes than any other HBCU in the nation. Some noteworthy athletes include Willis Reed, James Harris, and Doug Williams.

In 2013, members of Grambling State University football refused to play, resulting in the university being fined $20,000 by the Southwestern Athletic Conference. Grambling State University also faced a lawsuit from Jackson State University for failing to play in their homecoming contest. Jackson State University had to cancel a number of homecoming activities that were planned well in advanced, resulting in a significant local economic impact for the city of Jackson, Mississippi. Grambling's players staging the boycott accused university leaders of failure to fulfill their athletic scholarship obligations. Due to rundown facilities, long bus trips to road games and personnel decisions, there were many problems. They feared that if no one said anything, nothing would come of the institution.

Prior to the Jackson State University SWAC Conference game, Grambling University and Alcorn State University football teams played in the Circle City Classic, an annual HBCU football game held in Indianapolis, Indiana. The game sponsor provides each of the institutions funds to transport the respective teams. Alcorn State University decided to fly their teams and school officials, while Grambling University decided to place their team on charter buses for an eighteen-plus hour road trip. However, the president and athletic director from Grambling University flew.

Former Grambling President, Dr. Frank Pogue said at a press conference that Grambling players would not face any repercussions for the boycott, and that the national attention would help publicize the funding plight of HBCUs like Grambling. According to President Pogue, the university is committed to improving conditions of the football team by upgrading facilities. Grambling has endured a 57% cut in state funding over several years that has affected the entire campus. That year, the university president asked the athletic department to cut $335,000 from its overall department budget of $6.8 million. School spokesman Will Sutton said football was cut by $75,000 to about $2 million. Other critical issues surrounding the university athletic facilities included reports of mold in the locker rooms and improperly cleaned uniforms increasing the likelihood of staph infections. Local health department inspectors recommended improving the conditions.

Despite the possibility of losing their scholarship, members of the Grambling State University football team mounted a boycott during the year of 2013. The Grambling players refuse to return to practice until University President Pogue agreed to a full-scale review of the entire university to ensure that student health and safety was not being compromised. The boycott efforts by a group of black student athletes should serve as a wake-up call for not just the nation's most outstanding HBCU athletic program, but for all HBCUs. During the 2013 season, Grambling lost its first eight games. The school with such a rich winning tradition recorded a dismal (0–8) record. From 2012 to 2013, Grambling went through three coaches, and they have had four different directors of athletics from 2010 to present.

Members of the Grambling football team filed a letter of complaint with the Grambling administration. They cited that the athletic complex was in horrible and unsafe condition and was a hazard to their overall health. Unsafe conditions included mold and mildew on the floor, walls and ceiling. Players reported that their uniforms were poorly cleaned and there missing tiles in the weight room. When the dust cleared, the Grambling football team rebounded to its national status in black college sports, and President Pogue is no longer at Grambling. Did the football team and student population family get him fired for how he and his administration provided its students with unhealthy and unsafe conditions? President Pogue was not at all popular with the Grambling family. President Pogue had fired Doug Williams the most well-known sports figure in Grambling history. To complicate matters, Doug's son was the quarterback on the football team. President Pogue's tenure at Grambling was very interesting.

CHAPTER FOUR

The Sociopolitical Culture of Black-Athletes and Coaches

"And all Negroes at some period of their lives there is that yearning
for a sense of group unity that is the yearning of men for a flag:
for a unity that cannot be compromised, that cannot be bought;
that is conscious of itself, of its strength, that is militant."

—Ralph Ellison

This chapter examines the various ways in which the urban streets and environment have reshaped the culture of and constructs of sports. This chapter will also discuss what former first-round NBA pick Stephon Marbury describes as the politics or the politicks of professional sports, particularly how the NBA and NFL seek to promote forms of urban black culture to enhance the visibility and profit margins of their leagues. Despite ushering in some forms of urban black culture, both leagues have done a great job at policing the level of blackness throughout both leagues. The overall lived experiences of far too many black male athletes continue to be haunted by issues surrounding their racial formation or identification. To truly examine the social culture, a discussion about the social constructs of the black male athlete is warranted. What are the general characteristics of the black athlete? How are they viewed by nonblack consumers, and how are they wired mentally and physically? The culture of sports in America has blossomed into a popular commercial business based upon racial identity representation for both blacks and whites. Take, for example, both the NBA and the NFL; these two major-league sporting organizations are overwhelmingly represented by black males, just as the prison–industrial complex houses too many blacks under the age of thirty.

Both the NBA and NFL have done a pretty good job at managing and controlling the behavior of their prized black athletes. Truth be told, both leagues have put a lot of effort into presenting black male athletes as safe for white consumption. The majority of the profits earned by both leagues are based on the consumption habits of white fans, and these two leagues are preoccupied with raking in the money. At the end of the day, it is all about the money. Profits are the keys that keep the doors open for the sports industrial complex where so many black athletes are corralled mentally and physically day in and day out. Far too many black male athletes have a great deal negative baggage, and their imagination has been handicapped and in some cases even trapped in the world of their lived experiences based on a postindustrial ghetto lifestyle. As younger and younger players are joining the NFL and NBA, so has the urban street culture that S. Craig Watkins describes as ghettocentrism. The ghettocentric lifestyle of urban black athletes has become deeply rooted in the black athlete's psyche. Some aspects of the ghettocentrism have been repackaged and promoted in the same manner that old-school black cinema was packaged for specific audiences based on race and class. The term *ghettocentrism* refers to a style-driven culture of blackness defined by crude stereotypes. To better understand the ghettocentrism paradox, one must understand the interrelated themes present in the sports world (postindustrial and post-Fordism) that embody the symbolic limitation and risk of the contemporary urban landscape.

Understanding and dealing with the social construct of the black athlete's identity is very challenging. Understanding how the black athlete develops an understanding of social self is the first step. Athletic competition involving blacks was and still is an integral part of American and black cultures. It is not uncommon to see black athletes in television commercials selling products. You can listen to them on the radio selling products, and you can even see them projected on huge billboards. One might say that the bigger-than-life status that black stars possess is equal to fast-food industry's "Supersize It" mantra. Through slick marketing and packaging, the black athlete has become the "super black athlete" who can physically dominate their respective sports while large numbers of nonblacks are willing to pay a fee to be entertained.

In an excellent example, is how Dr. Todd Boyd's describes how blacks dominate basketball and have changed the culture of sports. He further states that blacks own the sports on one level, but the owners are in control. My analysis will look at all sports in which today's black athletes actively participate or have shown a serious interest. Even today the black athlete continues to struggle with race, class, politics, identity, and masculinity despite having millions of dollars and extensive public exposure. It is important to note that the year is 2017; we are less than sixty years removed from segregation. Like many other parts of society, sports were segregated. Many postindustrial black urban communities continue to produce a large number of black athletic stars who are eager to become the newest commodity or object for mass consumption among white fans who are more than willing to pay to see a safe, controlled, and nonthreatening black athlete preform.

Connecting ghettocentrism to professional sports and big-time intercollegiate sports is directly linked to both postindustrialism and post-Fordism in that they complement each other. As the use and inference of ghettocentrism came to be more relevant in the professional-sports world, so did the policing strategies being employed in poverty-stricken urban crime- and drug-infested communities. In many of these communities, the crime rates, drug problems and intense poverty all dictate a strict course of behavioral control. Over the years, we have all witnessed an even greater social breakdown within urban and rural communities that are producing black male athletes for the college and professional ranks. Within the context of the ghetto, the black male athlete is at further risk of becoming hypersegregated because of his actual lived experiences and the expressive values of his less than positive community of origin.

So what does that have to do with the psychological development of the average black male athlete from an urban or ghetto setting? The answer "Is a hell of a lot"; this is a lot for the young impressible mind to absorb. When all you see daily is menacing behaviors of crime, shooting, drug dealing, violence, and domestic abuse, coupled with living in less than desirable conditions, your mind is sure to play tricks on you. This should come as no surprise to anyone. Therefore, it should also come as no surprise that they continue to experience problems later in life in terms of their psychosocial development and adjustment to newer and better environments. The cognitive development of many young black athletes in urban and some rural settings has been compromised by their limited exposure to positive environments whereby they can develop the necessary mental and social attitudes needed to rise above the underclass black world that has failed to nurture them properly.

Jackie Robinson broke the color barrier, but he played in front of white fans. Blacks were only able to listen to the game on the radio. Jackie Robinson had the entire black community in the palm of his hand: He had made it to the *Show*. The Show is what they called the National Baseball League. When you make it to the Show, you have made it. By today's societal standards and cultural struggles, we would call this person the "Showman Negro," while rappers may make the analogy "Da Showman Nigga" by Dorrough Music. Dorrough carefully describes the struggles associated with being a "Showman Nigga." People pay to see you perform and act a certain way. In this case, he is describing the showman nigga as the modern-day controlled showman nigga. During the Jackie Robinson era, he would be described as the "Showman Negro more for white patrons than for black patrons. So, is it safe to say that today's black athlete is the new version of the "Showman Negro"? Is the black athlete the official showman? They have been allowed to entertain sports patrons with whatever skills they possess. Today's contemporary black athlete, as in the past, is almost guaranteed to fill seats for the owners.

Being that showman the black athlete today can be a serious struggle. The continued hustling struggle associated with race, class, politics, identity, and masculinity all may haunt the black athlete. The black athlete is seemingly loved by both blacks and whites, but we all know that love is subjective. Take, for example, Wade, Bosh, James and Durant. In the Hip-Hop culture, they would be called the "Showman Niggas." This is not to disrespect any of the four, but let's be honest. These four blacks fill seats for the all the NBA owners each time they hit the floor. They sell millions in products associated with the NBA. We all love Michael Jordan; he was a certified showman black athlete. At the end of his career he became a superior, highly paid, showman black athlete who is now a majority NBA owner. This too can be said about other great black athletes like Jackie Robinson, Jim Brown, Julius Erving, Earvin "Magic" Johnson, and the late, great Walter Payton just to name a few. Back in the 1980s, Earvin "Magic" Johnson and his LA Lakers team proclaimed to the Americas that the Lakers were "Showtime." Four black players and one Clark Kent eyeglass-wearing white guy would do the very same thing that Wade, Bosh or James did, fill seats for the all of the NBA owners.

Everybody wanted to see "Showtime," which just happened to be led by a 6'-9" black point guard named Earvin "Magic" Johnson. For some time now, blacks have been dreaming and hoping for a positive exchange in terms of landing the multimillion-dollar contacts. Despite the ghettocentric cultural practices, black urban and rural athletes have been able to develop a set of negotiation skills necessary to survive life's challenges. These practices include music, lifestyle, visual arts, and sporting activities.

Better connecting the black athlete to the postindustrial concept is quite simple. Opportunities are increasingly becoming limited as more and more black males have chosen sports as a career. Do the numbers in both leagues, the NBA and NFL, show just how many jobs are really out there? The NBA and NFL have only a few jobs each year, the level of competition is fierce. Too many black urban boys and even rural boys in the black community are depending on football or basketball as their way out of a bad situation. Many of these athletes feel as though there is are too few opportunities for them to achieve a sense of worth and success outside of athletics. Urban youth see two ways out of the ghetto: rappers or ballers. They see the potential of capital accumulation at an early age. They are like a deer trapped in a car's headlights. The highly developed athletic bodies, coupled with the talents of the ghettocentric athletes, make them prime potential product for diverse consumers.

Urban and rural youth from challenging underserved communities are often offered the notion of working hard as a means of relocating to a more desired community. Oftentimes, the athlete will embrace the concept in a one-dimensional manner. Most, if not all, of the hard work is directed towards their sports and less attention is placed upon academics and education. The majority of black athletes fail to work hard for positive academic success in the classroom. This often leaves them unqualified to function properly when their athletics careers end or, for some, never get off the ground. Believe it or not there are some great players who were just as good as Dwyane Wade, but could not get out of the streets of Chicago despite begin good enough to play in the NBA. Another relevant and popular theme that continues to resonate is the exploits and commodification of the black athlete's body as a form of natural raw materials as in the prison–industrial complex. Both the NBA and NFL have adopted the same prison–industrial-complex mentality as both leagues seek to recruit potential revenue-producing black athletes from uncaring, wild-style landscapes of the urban ghetto or poor rural communities in the south where drugs and crime have become the employment options for the majority.

Postindustrial forces have introduced the world to the black athletic industrial complex where vested interests maintain access to the newest and finest black product, the athlete. These leagues are fully committed to ensuring that an array of ghettocentric black athletes are available for public consumption by blacks and nonblacks alike, whoever is willing to pay for the pleasure. Echoing the lyrics of the Notorious Biggie Smalls, "Either you got a wicked jump short or you deal the crack rock," because that is the only way up and out of this ghetto we know as our home. There is a clear connection between modern-day black crime, the black-athlete, Hip-Hop culture, and the music that keeps the culture alive. The mainstream commercialization of the ghettocentric practices and images of Hip-Hop culture is worthy of exploration within the context of the black male athlete. The exceptional hard-working black male athletes represent the industrial ghetto communities or poverty stricken rural communities that produce one after another black male athlete like an assembly line for the Ford Motor Company. The real question is whether the assembly line or the industrial ghetto communities are over polluting the market with a product not yet ready for the intense commercialization associated with professional sports and big-time college athletics. We may want to brace ourselves for a recoil soon, as many of these young black males have the bodies, but their overall development lacks the psychosocial skills they need to run the race for life.

To further the discussion about ghettocentrism, Hip-Hop culture and sports, we must first understand that the ghettocentrism marketing can best be described as a fresh new approach that incorporates relevant themes representing specific styles, behaviors, values, and street language into a commodity with a symbolic capital value. Ghettocentrism strategies have for some time been used to market and promote an atmosphere for the packaging and handling of the black product in the form of black-athletes. In terms of currency, black is the new green in the sport-cultural economy. At the heart of the marketing themes associated with ghettocentrism and urbanism is not authenticity, but the overall appearance of authenticity that the black-athlete brings to the discussion. The continued commercial exploitation of young black life in the form of ghettocentrism and Hip-Hop culture has, for some time now, been motivated by the acknowledgement and fascination with the black product (the black-athlete), which equates to a positive revenue stream.

From 2005 to the present, ghettocentrism has proven to be profitable for the NBA year in and year out. The league is raking in billions through the multimedia commercial exploitation of a new fresh crop of the black product (the black-athlete) from the urban jungle. Each year, the league is eager to bring in a mixture of young talent from the urban underclass world. They are then pimped out or leased out for high financial gains. It is important to note that the NBA is not the only industry making money from the product. The product is more than often packaged with other corporate products such as cars, clothes, fast food, financial institutions, computers, and even computer games resulting in large profits for major white corporations. So again, we can see that black is the new green.

Despite the fact that he is an old dude, in basketball years, Michael Jordan is still taking in tons of money thanks largely to his deal with Nike to produce the Nike Jordan Brand line of sporting gear: hats, shoes, socks, shirts, and so on. Of course, there are new group hot dudes in basketball today: LeBron James, Dwyane Wade, Carmelo Anthony, and Kevin Durant. These four guys occupy prime space on the commercially engineered assembly line constructed to effectively market the newest black product to its consumer. All four have unlimited earning potential and will make even more for the league and corporate sponsors because they understand the value of incorporating aspects of urban street culture to better promote, market, and sell the black product, not just to blacks, but to nonblacks for entertainment consumption.

It is noteworthy that Anthony, James, and Durant are all products of single-parent homes. Their mothers did anything and everything they could for the betterment of their sons. They made sacrifices time after time so that their sons would one day amount to something special. Look at them all, they have done well despite their negative and challenging childhood and adolescent years. The conditions of the communities in which all of these young men came from were similar, though some may be more rough and dangerous than others. The toxic and unhealthy black communities reinforced nothing but tons of hopelessness on the horizon for far too many young black athletes. Anthony grew up in Baltimore's worst crime and drug-ridden community of West Baltimore. James was also raised in the poverty-stricken economically depressed Akron, Ohio, where crime and drugs were the main source of survival for most blacks his age. Kevin Durant also had to deal with challenging limitations of the urban jungle in which he was raised by a single mother, who he described as his MVP when he accepted the 2014 MVP award. Durant attributes all of his success to the sacrifices his mother made for him and his siblings. Dwyane Wade was raised in the rough and tough streets of Chicago, with one of the highest mortality rate for blacks.

Durant, James, Wade, and Anthony are all products of wounded communities and have amazed the world with their athletic skills and contemporary urban-ghetto authenticity, which continues to promote a climate for lucrative revenue gains in the mainstream marketplace. Next, we examine the ghettocentrism's and Hip-Hop's historical influences on the NBA and the NFL.

The National Basketball League

The NFL and NBA are overrepresented in terms of employing highly paid black industrial laborers and a few high-paid black overseers to assist with the controlling. Both professional leagues and big-time college football and basketball programs have successfully utilized the media to, first, bridge to the interested nonblack consumer and, second, normalize the relationship with white fans and corporate sponsors to demonstrate that the industrially built black athletes are hardworking and safe for consumption. It is important to note that the commodification of rural and urban industrially built black athletic bodies has tremendous commercial appeal to blacks and nonblack sports fans.

We must not lose sight of the rocky relationship between the black athlete and the communities that produced them in terms of general public perceptions. For example, basketball for some time now has become the game of choice for most blacks. Clearly, over the years, the game of basketball has become more and more a black game; the game is now dominated by black players since the league was first integrated by the likes of Jackie Moore, Earl Lloyd, and Chuck Cooper. Over the years, both the NBA and the NFL have carefully managed and marketed the ghettocentric attitudes and behaviors of their black athletes, thus capitalizing on the black product to the fullest in the post-Johnson–Bird and then the Jordan era. It is important to note that Jordan's blackness helped to create and further establish a huge financial windfall for the NBA and the league's corporate partners. The commodification of today's young black athletes has produced yet another cultural commercial financial outlet based solely on race.

Those outside of the both leagues have come to realize that incorporating specific aspects of ghettocentrism associated with the black athletes yields huge profits. Therefore it should be no surprise that Hollywood would get on board as they openly acknowledged the commercial value of incorporating various ghettocentric images of black culture. Such movies as *Boyz n the Hood, New Jack City,* and *He's Got Game* all successfully embraced and engaged the young black audience as the movie makers were able to capitalize on America's blackness. Following in the footsteps of Hollywood, both the NBA and NFL have successfully capitalized on their black product's ghettocentric baggage. Within the context of pro sports, mainly basketball and football, it has become damn near impossible to avoid the various ghettocentrism associated with black culture. Managing and marketing ghettocentrism to those outside of black communities has seemingly resulted in an effective promotional campaign for both leagues.

A prime example of ghettocentric rhetoric is Allen Iverson's entrance into the NBA in the mid-1990s. Iverson's home community was less than warm, safe, and inviting. Like many high-profile black athletes, he was raised by a single black mother. Prior to enrolling at Georgetown University, Iverson served jail time for alleged involvement in an interracial bowling alley fight in his hometown of Hampton, Virginia. During Iverson's two years at Georgetown University, coach John Thompson was apparently able to keep Iverson's ghettocentric values and behaviors under control and further served a positive male figure for the young basketball player.

However, once Iverson became a professional athlete, he seemed to change altogether. Iverson joined the Philadelphia 76ers in 1996, and the various layers of his ghettocentric upbringing began to emerge. Allen Iverson was the leader of the pack, with his tattoos and signature cornrow hair style. Allen was portrayed as a gangsta baller for the NBA's Philadelphia 76ers. The realism of his street-culture authenticity was offered up for public consumption. Iverson brought to the NBA his personal ghettocentrism, coupled with his distinguishing street-like and thuggish playing style, thus making him a contemporary embodiment of black culture authenticity. Reebok, one the NBA's corporate sponsors, quickly jumped on the Iverson train by signing him to a forty-million-dollar endorsement contract and was quick to provide Iverson with a signature shoe branded "The Answer," before he played his first game.

In a similar vein, John Wall of the Washington Wizards was recently given a similar deal with Reebok: twenty-five million dollars for five year before he played his first NBA game. Most recently, Wall just inked a new deal with Adidas, joining fellow NBA players Derrick Rose and Dwight Howard. Both Rose and Wall brought to the league some of the same characteristics as Iverson. Thanks to a variety of culturally based advertising campaigns, companies like Reebok and Adidas have earned billions based on modern day contemporary black culture. While Iverson is no longer in the NBA, current players like Wall and Rose are both prime examples of the controlled and managed commodification of black authenticity that is packaged and marketed to both white and black fans who are somewhat fascinated with images of ghettocentric behaviors.

We now move ahead in the discussion by examining the big three: LeBron James, Dwyane Wade and Carmelo Anthony. These three also arrived in the NBA with a ghettocentric pedigree. All three now occupy the prime space in the NBA in terms of endorsements that are deeply rooted in their authentic black culture. Various corporate NBA sponsors have successfully borrowed from the lifestyles and rugged urban landscapes where James, Wade and Anthony all grew up by promoting well-crafted and commercially engineered engagement opportunities including ghettocentric black discourse. The seductive characteristic of what many describe as ghetto authenticity continues to offer lucrative cultural capital within the commercial marketplace. The NBA and its corporate sponsors have profited tremendously from the promotion of its teams' efforts and, specifically, its high-valued players with their street culture and its ability to sell tickets and merchandise to nonblacks.

The National Football League

The NFL, despite being nearly 80% black, continues to maintain a strong connection and appeal to the non-black white-collar working class. The NFL continues to hold the interest of hard-working blue-collar industrial white men. At the start of the twentieth century, when football was yet another sport reserved for elite white college males, it was considered to be a rite of passage that fostered leadership, character, and masculine traits of toughness. Football, unlike basketball, has emerged as the rational industry that has become accustom to depending on the labor and entrainment that many postindustrial playgrounds are producing. The NFL's main audience was once largely centered in such Midwest cities as Saint Louis, Chicago, and Cleveland and such East Coast cities as Pittsburg, New York, and Boston with their large urban blue-collar populations. However, today the demographics have shifted somewhat to include the South, West Coast, and Southwest.

For some time now the NFL has been ushering in more and more young black males who were born under the umbrella of Hip-Hop culture. Many of these young black players are entering the league lacking the necessary social development and discipline. The NFL has drawn a line in the sand. It will not tolerate menacing criminal or drug-related behaviors from anyone playing and representing this league. The NFL has always been more resistant than other leagues to putting black styles of behavior on exhibit for general public consumption. The NFL and football in general, has always been deeply rooted in the Caucasian culture of sports. The NFL has done a good job of aggressively self-policing the league and its black players in a manner designed to repress the cultural encroachment and social development of the black football player. The cultural footprints are relevant in terms of the traditional white culture space, whereby white control remains the number-one priority. The NFL truly embodies the legitimate white notion of vision and privilege, by which the game is governed, controlled, and understood.

Nonetheless, the NFL has excelled at exploiting the black athlete for positive financial gain. The league is not afraid to render sanctions or suspension to anyone in danger of breaking the white-imposed laws established by the league office and the white owners in control. Consider the Josh Gordon story and the Carolina Panther defensive end, Greg Hardy. Josh Gordon was arrested around 3 a.m. on a Saturday for DWI in Raleigh, North Carolina. Gordon, who had led the NFL with 1,646 yards in the previous season, appealed a suspension for the 2014 season for his third violation of the substance-abuse policy. He had reportedly tested positive for marijuana in the latest violation. In May, Gordon was stopped for speeding and one of the three passengers in his car was in possession of marijuana. Sources with four NFL clubs indicated that Gordon had failed three drug tests while in college. The first two came at Baylor. The second, according to these sources, came after charges were dropped in his marijuana-related arrest of 2010, and that led to his dismissal from the private Baptist school, which has a reputation for being tough on drugs. That led to his transfer to Utah, where he failed a third test.

Greg Hardy, a former Carolina Panther, was found guilty of communicating threats to and assaulting his then girlfriend. The Hardy case came on the heels of another high-profile case by a star player. A Baltimore Ravens running back and his then fiancée (now wife) were arrested and charged for allegedly striking each other in an Atlantic City casino. Having one of the league's star players found guilty of putting his hands on a woman is not a good look. Carolina Panthers star, Greg Hardy, was ordered to surrender his ten guns as part of a judge's order after the guilty verdict. Greg Hardy's legal troubles should come as no surprise. During the 2010 pre-draft workouts, several NFL teams asked if he was bipolar. It was perhaps largely due to off field concerns while he was playing college football at Ole Miss. During the 2007 season, he was suspended indefinitely for missing team meetings. He was reinstated two weeks later after subsequent apologies to both coaches and reporters. One week after a dominating performance against the defending national champion, the Florida Gators, during the 2008 season, the defensive end was benched midway through a loss to South Carolina for what his coaches described as poor performance and athletic intensity on the field. He seemed to have no solid answer to defend his behavior on and off the field except to guardedly reply, "I'm not crazy, but you walk into a room and the first thing NFL scouts are asking is about your mental health." Hardy quickly became frustrated when potential teams continued to ask the same question. NFL teams also seemed to have no solid answer to the Greg Hardy question, which caused him to fall all the way to the 175th pick, winding up, of course, with the Carolina Panthers and earning $13.1 million for the 2014 season after being suspended for its entirety.

The NFL is less tolerant then the NBA. They are intent on punishing athletes for seeking to stand out and present a sense of individual style or engage in any form of self-expressive celebratory behaviors considered to be a threat against the perceived sanctity of white working class industrial values. The NFL has instituted a set of rules specifically intended for black players. However, the NFL does allow some players, under their strict approval and guidance, the ability to participate in consumer marketing to enhance media exposure.

The NFL has not been by any means a slow leak in the pursuit of revenue profits, largely because the league has calculated carefully and engaged in conservative movement that generate both interest and revenue while still preserving its blue-collar normative white culture. As more and more Hip-Hop-culture players have joined the NFL as players, fans' and commercial partners' opinions have begun to change.

The tense relationship between the NFL, the NBA, and Hip-Hop culture, as well as popular culture's ability to promote a crystallized representation of black men within the context of urban street culture, will only further reinforce a specific set of behavior problems based on race value. Black NFL players who cannot follow league rules have been labeled by the league as potential trouble makers and even potential troops of Hip-Hop culture hedonism seeking to change the league's rules at halftime. The close normative lifestyle many black athletes maintain with gang culture, and even drug dealers has the league on high alert. The league's ability to effectively market black athletes has resulted in an influx of younger NFL players with ghetto upbringings and socializations. The league's overall thinking about the cross connection of Hip-Hop and the NFL has the league more concerned about Hip-Hop cultural baggage. The NFL is seemingly less concerned that its players in the league have guns. The real issue is that so many of these young blacks not only might have a gun, but many have multiple gun, as did former Carolina Panther star Greg Hardy.

The NBA has made extensive efforts to carefully manage its racial order by paying more attention to its players' ghettocentric culture. In contrast, the NFL has placed more emphasis on enforcing rules to deal the ghettocentric underpinnings of its players. The NFL, despite its abundance of black bodies, is based on the blue-collar white sports community. Unlike basketball, which is more rooted in what can be described as a postindustrial urban blackness, football has perhaps maintained an attachment to a blue-collar industrial white community. Despite the increasing number of black players, football has traditionally always been reserved for whites. To say that the NFL has less quickly embraced ghettocentric behaviors is somewhat of an understatement. Within the context of racial coding in the NFL, black athletes have been concurrently overexploited for financial gains and yet fined by the league office for inappropriate behaviors including violence and drug-related offenses as a measure the entrenched fear of black players who break or abuse the white-imposed rules that govern the game of football. Such fines and penalties for unwanted behaviors seemingly provide a public exhibition of the power and control of whites in a position of authority.

Unlike the NBA, the NFL has adopted stiffer rules for its players, mainly its black players. Most recently, the NFL considered banning the use of the N-word by the league's players, which is deeply rooted in the ghettocentric authenticity of the majority of the league's black players. This word is so common that many players in both the NFL and NBA use it daily. Black players in the NFL and people in general regularly use it to describe their relationship among friends. It seems a bit much for the NFL to prohibit the use of this word which truly a part of the black players ghettocentric roots. It is important to note that many black NBA and NFL players have deeply rooted values associated with Hip-Hop cultural rituals. The NFL and NBA have become yet another outlet for Hip-Hop to expand its reach outside the black community.

Black-athletes who have gotten caught up in the ghettocentric web and the Hip-Hop culture have given the NBA and NFL owners, coaches, and league officials reasonable grounds to enforce strict conduct rules or simply seek out players who are less likely to bring to the league ghettocentric or Hip-Hop values.

Truly the NBA was much more willing to capitalize on the Hip-Hop values and ghettocentric attributes of its black players. The NFL is now seemingly on board as they have begun to accept some forms of Hip-Hop culture and ghettocentric themes. Despite the changing cultural landscape in both the NBA and the NFL, the preoccupation and healthy consumptive appetite of white fans continue to rule. The white owners, coaches, and fans of the NBA and NFL have all become well-adjusted to the ghettocentric blackness associated with the Hip-Hop marketing machine despite the potential problems that many of these black athletes bring to the leagues. Furthermore, the increasingly pervasive ghettocentric themes and Hip-Hop culture are historically tied to the racial fears and concerns of many white spectators. However, there is still a real fascination among many white spectators who are seeking entertainment and simply view blacks as those who are controlled, managed, and manipulated by the white owners and coaches. Ultimately, the ghettocentric themes and Hip-Hop culture associated with the black athletes based on the black bodies and the black product represent nothing less than a new landscape to be colonized by the corporate capitalist in both the NBA and NFL.

The urban rhetoric of the streets and the embodiment of ghettocentrism is deeply rooted in the majority of urban black athletes who make it to college and the professional ranks. Many black professional stars have openly acknowledge that, prior to signing that first contract, their lives and lived experiences had been really hard and stressful. The circumstances of living in single-parent homes with their mothers and often multiple siblings, little or no food some times, and even homelessness are well reported. True, this has not been then case for all black sporting stars: Both Michael Jordan and Grant Hill came from two-parent homes, as did Chris Weber and Magic Johnson. In the mid-1990s, the NBA took notice that things were changing and its chief product, the black athlete, was driving the change. Suddenly the NBA was faced with the dilemma of how to preserve the integrity of the league, but also to continue to market its number-one commodity to white fans and corporate sponsors. It was virtually impossible to avoid the ghettocentric themes of urbanism while effectively promoting the culture of commercial basketball. Some of the more notable black players of the 1990s helped introduce the ghettocentric themes of urban communities to the NBA and it corporate sponsors and helped develop culture-specific urban marketing and promotional campaigns for nonblack consumers.

All one has to do is take some time and watch any of the Nike commercial that features a black NBA or NFL player and you will see the richness of the ghettocentric urban brand. Both professional leagues and even some colleges and universities have profited immensely from the creative promotion and marketing of celebrity players who are more than willing to use their past as a bridge to financial gains. Despite the willingness to accept the menacing behaviors of black athletes, the NFL, NBA, and colleges are quick to police and enforce the rules against any behaviors that may impact their healthy images. It is important to note that when one of their players steps out of line, you can be assured that they will be dealt with quickly to clearly show the general public that they are more than willing to control the product, often issuing large financial fines. A number of governing rules have been put in place by professional leagues directly addressing the potential menacing behaviors of the black-athlete. These rules are aimed solely at better managing and controlling the young black athletes now entering the leagues in droves. Both leagues are unwilling to let anyone bring any negative attention to the league with unwanted menacing behaviors. The leagues are more than willing to allow these young black athletes to join the professional ranks and generate public interest based on cultural differences despite high levels of continued racial anxiety across society.

Beyond the NFL and the NBA, both Nike and Under Armor have managed to balance their relationship with black athletes and their culture to mobilize nonblack consumers. The NBA has out raced the NFL in exploiting the ghetto lifestyle and upbringing of the black athlete. More recently the NFL's promotional approaches have been more in tune with the ghettocentric themes and Hip Hop culture when marketing to the mainstream blue-collar whites. Both the NFL and NBA are fully committed to playing nice and engaging the ghettocentric urban logic as a means of promoting valuable products and services. The black athletes disconnection from the black community and the retaliation black athletes often face from the reactionary sports media has fractured the common cause that once united all black athletes ability to stand up and speak out for justice.

Coaches

In 2008, Charles Barkley openly accused Auburn of race discrimination. Auburn hired Gene Chizik over Turner Gill. According to Barkley, race was the deciding factor. It is important to note that black head coaches continue to be statistically marginalized within the NCAA structure. There is a serious racial inequality in college athletic when it comes to coaching.

Next, we will briefly discuss the lack of black coaches in the two main sports where blacks are well represented (basketball and football). Until white university presidents and athletic directors make the effort to go against the "white only" policy, the discussion will continue. The most promising effort to date is the "pledge" by the NCAA Division I presidents to hire more coaches of color. This pledge was announced during the summer of 2016. Bernard Franklin, Vice President of the NCAA issued a letter stating the intent of the NCAA and the Division I presidents.

There is evidence of racism throughout the college and professional coaching ranks. It is important to remember that during the early days of the civil-rights struggles, many businesses justified not hiring blacks with arguments about their customers' racial preferences. They firmly maintained that racist whites would not buy from black salesmen or eat food served by black waiters. Could this be true for major white colleges and universities with respect to white boosters not fully supporting black coaches and athletic directors? Note that there is a hiring problem with black athletic directors, as well as general mangers' at the professional level.

This is not just a Jim-Crow South thing. Hiring policy for coaches is very problematic throughout college football. In 2008, there only six black coaches at the Division I level, out of 119 coaches, less than 6%. At the same time in the sport of basketball, the numbers were somewhat better; over a quarter of major college basketball coaches and nearly one quarter of NFL coaches were black.

It is time to sound the alarm on the lack of black college coaches. The former DePaul assistant and current Chicago State head coach has some concern about the future of his profession. Tracy Dildy grew up watching and idolizing black coaches like Nolan Richardson and John Thompson as they won NCAA championships. He now wonders if the African-American coach is becoming extinct. He is equally concerned that no one is paying attention to the lack of head coaching opportunities for blacks.

Central Florida's Institute for Diversity and Ethics in Sport noted that head coaching opportunities for people of color "declined significantly" in 2013–2014. Just 22% of men's Division I basketball coaches were black, down from 23% the year before. The best time to be a black basketball coach was 2005–2006 when 25.2% were African-American. The worst time according to The Institute for Diversity and Ethics in Sport was in 2011-12 when only 18.6% were black. The inequity was striking given that 58% of college basketball players were African-American and nearly every bench includes at least one black assistant. There is a talented group of hungry black assistant coaches who may never get that opportunity to become a head coach if the "white-first policy" continues.

College basketball was once the most diverse hiring ground for black coaches. However, some thirty years after John Thompson won a national title at Georgetown and some twenty years after Nolan Richardson did so for Arkansas, this road to opportunity has become less traveled by black men. Until 2014, no black coach won a national title after Tubby Smith did at Kentucky. Smith was only the third black coach in the history of the NCAA to take home the top prize in college basketball. However, over those years, four black coaches have reached the Final Four without winning: Mike Davis at Indiana in 2002, Paul Hewitt at Georgia Tech in 2004, John Thompson III at Georgetown in 2007, and Shaka Smart at Virginia Commonwealth in 2011. In 2014, Kevin Ollie became the fourth black coach to win a national Championship. Ollie, was a former Huskies player who served as an assistant for two years before taking over the program from Jim Calhoun. Kevin Ollie at one point during his career was the highest paid coach in the American Athletic Conference.

College basketball's shortage of coaching diversity is not just at the top-level institutions. It has been a recent trend throughout intercollegiate athletics. At the college level, when the conversation turns to hiring a black coach, the issue of race always seems to surface. The top-five power conference in 2015 had only 20% (13 of 65 coaches) overall blacks. The Big Ten had the smallest number of black coaches: only one former NBA player, Eddie Jordan at Rutgers, until he was replaced by a white coach. What is somewhat troublesome is that four schools (Illinois, Michigan State, Nebraska, and Purdue) have never hired a black head basketball coach. What is even more troublesome is that when race becomes the main variable, people seem to get somewhat uncomfortable and even nervous. The 2012 racial and gender report card for college sports, which was produced by Central Florida's Institute for Diversity and Ethics in Sport, indicated that the current pool of black Division I head coaches was only 18.6% through the 2011–2012 season. This is the lowest percentage since the 1995–1996 season. Another troublesome point is that for some time multiple administrators at the Division I, II, and III levels have seemingly passed up the opportunity to hire and promote black coaches at the same rate as white coaches.

The race issue in terms of the lack of black coaches remains incendiary. Very few college and university administrators are willing to seriously take on the discussion of why there are so few black coaches. It is unfortunate that the black coach dialogue makes so many white athletic directors, who represent nearly 90% at the Division I level, somewhat uncomfortable. It is equally important to note that, despite the Black Coaches Association, far too many black coaches are less willing to speak up for fear of being labeled rebels or militants. It is that level of hesitancy that continues to handicap black coaches, coupled with the unwillingness of white administrators to speak up and affirm their colleges' and universities' polices against discrimination and their efforts to encourage and hire black coaches. For far too many black coaches, these polices sound good on paper, but the numbers tell the truth. This problem continues to exist year after year, and the issue of too few black head coaches remains in the two top revenue-generating sports: football and basketball.

It is important to note that 57.2% of Division I men's basketball players are black, while black coaches represent less than 20%. Despite slight progress in the hiring of black men's basketball coaches, it seems that progress has slowed or stopped all together, which is very disappointing in a nation that prides itself on freedom, justice, and equality for all regardless of the color of one's skin. It is seemingly okay to hire a few black coaches, but not too many. Those in the decision-making apparatus have turned their backs on black coaches. There have been and continue to be many black assistant coaches, but their path to head-coaching positions is not an easily traveled one. In fact, if you are black, it is damn near impossible to jump from the rank of assistant coach to head coach.

Black coaches are merely seeking an opportunity; they are not seeking a hand out, just a fair opportunity. White administrators continue to hide behind the issue that black coaches lack head coaching experience and that race is not really the issue. However, the real deal is that far too many blacks cannot even get their foot in the door to gain the experience needed. Also concerning is that very few white coaches have any head coaching experience prior to their first head-coaching job. The perception and attitude of white administrators, athletic directors, and head coaches is that the black assistant coaches are great recruiters, but they lack the skills and personality needed to manage and ultimately run a program.

The truth of the matter is that black assistant coaches for the most part have seemingly hit a ceiling in college basketball. There must be in place a central way to change the current climate to truly create real avenues that will value black coaching candidates. The real deal is that the real decisions are usually being made a group of powerful men, and in some cases a few women, who are mainly white. They all want to win, and their job is to find a person who can do that. In most cases, it has been the white coaches who have been in the position to produce a win. At the major college level, job security for most athletic directors is often tied to the success of their most recent hires in the top sports. Therefore, the primary objective is to hire those they believe are best qualified candidates to succeed. This tends to handicap the black coaching candidate.

The issue of cultural differences also factors into the hiring process. White administrators will often rely on personal connections and recommendations from other white administrators. Another factor is that white administrators are seeking candidates who fit similar profiles and thrive in similar social and professional circles, which may further handicap or limit the opportunities for the minority candidate during the hiring process. Mark Daigneault, an assistant to Florida coach Billy Donovan who has studied treatment discrimination in men's college basketball coaching through the sports management program at the University of

Florida, describes the lack of black coach hires through the homologous-production theory. Daigneault suggests that people tend to surround themselves with those of similar races and backgrounds. The potential ramifications of that theory in collegiate sports tend to be a uniform athletic departments and coaching practice in play for years according to Daigneault. If the majority of administrators and coaches are white and they are more likely to network with and surround themselves with people like themselves, they are unlikely to hire people unlike themselves.

The SEC has become the nation's most diverse conference in Division I men's basketball. Seven of the league's head coaches are black and one is Hispanic. Former Oregon State basketball coach and brother-in-law to former President Obama, Craig Robinson says schools may need to cast a wider net when looking for black athletic leaders. No one seems to really have the correct answer. Maybe we should look to NIKE and *just do it*. That means hire more black coaches and give them an opportunity to either succeed or fail. The NCAA is not like the NBA and NFL. It is ultimately up to the NCAA membership institutions who must be committed to and agree to hiring more black coaches. Most people may not understand that the NCAA alone cannot enforce hiring policies at the institutional level. This process must begin at the top with the presidents, chancellors, and athletic directors.

Black Football Coaches by the Numbers

During the 2012 season, the 124 Division 1-A college football schools boasted only fifteen black coaches according to an executive report produced by the Black Coaches Association. The Big Ten conference has seen zero black head coaches in the past ten years. The head coach is definitely the most visible; however assistant coaches in support roles are equally underrepresented. Only 312 of the 1,018 college football assistant coaches are black and only thirty-one of 255 of college offensive and defensive coordinators are black. Combined, black football coaches and support staff represent a measly 5% of Football Bowl Subdivision numbers. At Division II and III schools, the numbers are even more devastating. The Black Coaches Association reported that, in the 2012 season, only nine schools in these two categories had head coaches of color. These numbers do not include HBCUs.

The Problem and the Solution

Despite the thousands of black college football players in recent decades, only a handful have been entrusted with opportunities to lead teams. Many of these former players obviously understand the game and have a strong knowledge of college-level football both on and off the field, yet the doors remain closed. So, what is the real problem? Why do black football coaches continue to be overlooked for coaching jobs? Some believe that the problem is that schools are quick to dismiss black coaches because they are black. Many critics are quick to note that white coaches with poor winning records are often still considered a hot commodity by other schools despite their win–loss records, but blacks are not measured by the same standards. If given the opportunity, black coaches have historically been given just one shot to prove what they can do. It is also important to note that a college football coach does not have the same responsibilities as an NFL coach. Winning at the college level is critical to the university. In fact, winning games may be more important than winning in the graduation rate. Winning games also plays an important and direct role in the institution's current revenue and its ability to generate revenue in future years by attracting new students and selling athletic merchandise.

Beyond a doubt, the numbers tell a stark truth about underrepresentation of blacks among football coaches at the college and professional levels. There is a real problem, and not just at the Division I level. The problem extends into Division II and III in the college system. Fortunately, the NBA, NFL, and MLB all continue to open the door wider for black coaches to enter and stay. With so much being said about this issue, it is unfortunate that little problem solving has occurred. It would serve colleges and university administrators well to take a cue from the NFL when it comes to hiring and promoting minority coaches. In 2003, the NFL introduced the Rooney Rule, which required NFL teams to interview at least one minority candidate for every vacant head coaching position and other executive football operation spots. After just three seasons, the Rooney Rule lead to a 22% increase across the board in the number of black head coaches in the NFL and those numbers rise every season. A similar rule for the college ranks would go a long way towards improving the opportunities for black coaches and athletic directors, especially in the context of higher education's so-called affirmative action programs to bolster diversity and opportunities.

Another possible solution would be to establish effective mentorship programs for minority coaches and athletic administrators. This would allow former players, coaches, and even those interested in a career in sports administration to then begin working their way through the athletic ranks, thus gaining valuable experience. Despite the NCAA's hands-off approach, these changes should be encouraged and supported by the NCAA for a real dynamic shift to be felt across the board. Every NCAA member institution should have the same diversity and affirmative-action opportunities. It is not enough that we talk about it; it is critical that we make sure that more NCAA institutions take a closer look at blacks to fill head football coaching roles.

Much of the attention has been on basketball, but the numbers in football are far worse. The 2014 college football season opened up with a total of eleven black Division 1 head coaches. Most prominent among them were Texas A&M's Kevin Sumlin, Charlie Strong of Texas, and Stanford's David Shaw. What is most interesting about these black coaches and where they coach is that they all are in states with fertile high school recruiting grounds: Texas and California. Both states produce copious college football recruits. Despite the efforts of Sumlin, Strong, and Shaw, Dr. Fitz Hill, President of Arkansas Baptist College and author of *Crackback! How College Football Blindsides the Hopes of Black Coaches*, feels there is more to do. The overall winning percentages of black football coaches tend to suffer because most black football coaches take over or inherit programs that require a major rebuilding process or have received NCAA sanctions. Furthermore, they are given little time to turn the program around before they are fired. Consequently, many have very low winning percentages, which results in many black coaches receiving a negative perception in reference to their coaching abilities and skills.

CHAPTER FIVE

The Academic Problem

"I'm not comfortable being preachy, but more people need to start spending as much time in the library as they do on the basketball court. If they took the idea that they could escape poverty through education, I think it would make a more basic and long-lasting change in the way things happen. What we need are positive, realistic goals and the willingness to work."

—Kareem Abdul-Jabbar

We must be open and honest about the issue of academic progress and student-athletes' progress towards graduation, particularly the black student-athlete. It is truly unfortunate that far too many of these highly skilled black athletes who are seen by millions and who have become major universities' and colleges' poster children do not stand a snowball's chance in hell of making it academically. According to an executive summary by the Graduate School of Education at the Penn Center for the Study of Race and Equity in Education, between 2007 and 2010, black men accounted for only 2.8% of full-time degree-seeking undergraduate students at the Division I level, yet they represented 57.1% of football teams and 64.3% of basketball teams. Across four yearly cohorts, only 50.2% of black male student-athletes and 55.5% of black undergraduate men went on to graduate within six years, compared to 66.9% of all student-athletes and 72.8% of undergraduate students overall. Even more amazing, 96.1% of NCAA Division I colleges and universities graduated black male student-athletes at rates lower than student-athletes overall and 97.4% of institutions graduated black male student-athletes at rates lower than undergraduate students overall. Furthermore, on 72.4% of Division I campuses, graduation rates for black male student-athletes were lower than rates for black undergraduate men overall.

The heart of the matter is that is that far too many black student-athletes are not obtaining their college degree, and far too many have failed to gain the preparation needed to establish a professional career beyond sports. Within the context of higher education, the goal is to grow and develop the minds of student-athletes in exchange for their athletic prowess. If we are failing to do so, then we have failed at the institutional level. There's no question that athletics can be a pathway to education that can transform lives. But all too often, black student-athletes leave college without degrees, and with little of the training they need to succeed in life beyond sports. So, how can we improve retention and graduation rates? We must continue shining a light on the issue and hope that more institutions and conferences will begin to pay real attention. More importantly, we must seek to address the important issue that will ultimately determine black student-athletes' futures. A more serious game plan for addressing and improving how institutions score more wins in educating black student-athletes is needed.

Key Steps for Improving Graduation Rates

First and foremost, college presidents, trustees, and faculty members must demand transparency and data from athletics departments and offices of institutional research. Presidents must hold themselves, athletic directors, and coaches accountable for narrowing graduation gaps. Coaches and athletic administrators must pay closer attention to their student-athletes' course enrollment and major selection. Our institutions must pay more attention to and examine ways to fully support postgraduation pathways such as graduate school, employment placement in the students' major fields of study, and even plan for recruitment of student-athletes into their own athletics departments when possible. Working with faculty members to raise their consciousness of negative stereotypes and assumptions is equally important. Additionally, assigning faculty mentors from outside the athletics department for these student-athletes can be very helpful in increasing their academic engagement and their likelihood of graduating.

Coaches and athletics departments should be required to provide a detailed plan for improving their athletes' educational outcomes. The goal is not only to get them through college, but to provide a foundation for productive careers after college. More transparency is needed if we are serious about changing the direction of black student-athletes' graduation rates. The overrepresentation of black male student-athletes is unlikely to surprise anyone who is a fan of NCAA football and men's basketball. This is even more true for scholars who have studied race in intercollegiate athletics recently. The racial inequities in the six-year graduation rates are seemingly more troublesome today. However, what is still shocking for some is that, while these trends are so pervasive, institutional leaders, including the NCAA and athletics conference commissioners, have not done more in response to them. Another astonishing factor is that the American public, most current and former black student-athletes, sports enthusiasts, journalists, and leaders in black communities seem to calmly accept the widespread inequities that continue to devalue educating black student-athletes on one hand while reproducing revenue-generating college sports programs on the other hand. What is even more outrageous is that no one in the black community is willing to throw a flag for the lack of accountability, which persistently keeps far too many disadvantage black male student-athletes playing catch up in a game that far too many will not finish at all. Surely, leaders in black communities, institutional leaders, and the NCAA should be able to define a clear path from the stadiums and gyms to the graduation stages.

The NCAA Academic Progress Rate (APR) is now starting to have a major impact on Division II conferences such as the CIAA and the SAIC. The graduation rates for CIAA institutions vary, with the public institutions leading the way in terms of student-athletes obtaining college degrees. Fayetteville State University, Elizabeth City State University, Virginia State University, and Winston-Salem State University all have favorable graduation rates ranging between 40 to 60%. In contrast, public Bowie State University alone among several private institutions (Chowan University, Johnson C. Smith University, Lincoln University of Pennsylvania, Livingstone College, Saint Augustine's University,

Shaw University, and Virginia Union University) struggles to graduate student-athletes. The NCAA now requires all institutions to disclose their graduation rates to prospective student-athletes and their families. Low-performing institutions with poor academic scores have student-athlete graduation rates as low as 19% to 33%.

Overall at the Division II level, the numbers were somewhat better, but they are not altogether great. Black athletes continue to struggle behind their white counterparts. Who is to blame for the black athlete's weak academic success at Predominately White Institutions (PWI) and even some Historically Black Colleges and Universities (HBCUs)? Truth be told, coaches, parents, and the student-athletes themselves must all share the blame in the overall academic failures of the black athlete. Coaches will go overboard convincing the admission office to get highly skilled black student-athletes admitted to college, knowing full well that the academic course load, the demands of intercollegiate sports, including travel, practice time, games, and postgame activities, will monopolize the majority of their time, leaving little time for academics. For coaches, it is all about winning; if that means forcing the hand of the admissions department at major universities with high academic standards to have that blue-chip athlete admitted, so be it. One of the more common lines focuses on the impact that this student-athlete is going to have on the university: We cannot afford to not admit the student-athlete, because they will not only sell tickets, but they also have the potential to assist with the recruitment of future student-athletes and non-student-athletes. This is a win–win situation, truly for the university and the coach. However, this is not necessarily good for the student-athlete in the end. It is important to note that it is not the just the coaches. Presidents and Chancellors are all involved in the progress when it comes to having a high-profile, successful athletic department. At the end of the day, many high-profile and successful university athletic programs are completely committed to investing and betting on the black student athletes. Over the years there has been a great economic return for Predominately White Institutions.

Parents may be the most significant players in the entire game. For eighteen years or more parents prepare the potential student-athlete with a solid foundation to deal with the challenges associated with academic success or a lack thereof. Again it is unfortunate that far too many student-athletes can compete at such a high level athletically, but can barely complete academically at the high school level. This is indeed criminal, and someone should be held accountable. Every parent wants their child to graduate from college, but far too many know that their child, if not for his athletic abilities, has no business at some of these major universities. In my research for this book, I read in Shawn Powell's powerful book that one parent told a coach who was recruiting her son to make sure that her son graduates. The coach's response was that he could not do what she failed to do in eighteen years. Was the coach wrong for telling the parent the truth?

It is the parents' responsibility to teach their children, whether they are budding superstars or not, to treat academics as the precious jewel it is. This must start very early, not during the freshman year in high school. Let us not forget the fourth-grade syndrome proposed by Dr. Jawanza Kunjufu. At this age, boys in black homes experience a decline in parental involvement and an increase in peer pressure. He further notes that there are declines in nurturing and teacher expectations. At this age, athletics jumps ahead of academics. The black student-athlete must have the same desire and intensity for academic as for athletics. Winning in the classroom is critical for the survival of black athletes after their legs, arms, and knees are no longer able to carry them. In the words of Dr. Benjamin E. Mayes, "Education is the passport to the future." Helping the black student understand and conceptualize this passage as early as possible is the parent's most important task, especially during crucial early developmental and elementary years. We must teach our children to value academics over athletics. Today, despite all of the horror stories about athletes down on their luck after having great athletic careers, far too many black athletes are still willing to gamble it all for the opportunity to shoot that basketball, run that football, or try to knock another black or white athlete out on the football field. They are willing to bet it all on sports, focusing very little on the academic end; far too many parents sit on the sidelines cheering their babies on.

The student-athlete must also assume some ownership in their overall success outside of athletics. Yes, parents and coaches are critical players, but it is ultimately the student-athletes' responsibility to perform both academically and athletically. At the end of the day, student-athletes must demand to be treated as students who want to achieve academically.

At the Division II level, the Presidents Council has established "Life in the Balance," a philosophy that calls for a comprehensive program of learning and development for all student-athletes in an effort to improve graduation rates at the Division II level. This philosophy provides growth opportunities through academic achievement, learning in high-level athletics competition, and development of societal attitudes in service to community. The balance and integration of these different areas of learning opportunity provide Division II student-athletes with a path to graduation while seeking to develop critical life skills and knowledge for life beyond sports. Division II has taken a significant step toward the student-athlete by endorsing "Life in the Balance" legislation to reduce the number of athletic contests, thus refocusing more emphasis on academics.

Still today, many black athletes are leaving high school headed to college completely unprepared to successfully navigate college life, particularly the academic world associated with intercollegiate athletics. The day has come for black student-athletes to attend college on athletic scholarships. However, they have totally failed to perfect the basic academic achievement beyond middle school, let alone high school. The real question has become, can they function at the college level if they are reading at the middle school level. Black athletes have been given a passing grade for years on the academic end in exchange for their athletic performances, skills, and abilities, but those grades will not give them the skills they will need when those abilities fail to take them to the top.

These stories are all too common in the two major sports where the black athletes continue to dominate, basketball and football. There is enough blame for coaches, parents, and student-athletes to share. It is unfortunate that a disproportionate number of black student-athletes are being used and discarded by major universities. In *Soul Out*, Powell sums it up best. For the most part, college coaches know damn well that these student-athletes cannot handle the academic challenges that have been established by these institutions, not to mention the NCAA. From the coach's standpoint, their solution to the problem is to provide the student-athlete with academic counselors and tutoring; which would be great if they helped the student learn. Unfortunately, these counselors and tutors are doing more than providing academic support and tutoring. Consequently, the black student-athlete continues to struggle academically.

Another trend on major college campuses is to place the black student-athlete into academic programs less traveled by higher achieving non-athletes. Programs where you are likely to find the black student-athlete include sports management, hotel management, restaurant management, sociology, criminal justice, and black studies just to name a few. In addition, many athlete departments have special arrangements with many of these departments for their student-athletes. It is not uncommon for many student-athletes to not even attend class at all or regularly. Most recently, the NCAA came down hard on the University of North Carolina at Chapel Hill for major infractions involving their football team. The NCAA investigation was launched after a probe into improper benefits and academic misconduct revealed embarrassing irregularities and suspect classes in an academic department, with football players making up more than a third of enrollments in those classes. This is a prime example of weak institutional control. The investigation also found fraud and poor oversight in fifty-four classes in the Department of African and Afro-American Studies between the summer of 2007 and the summer of 2011. That included unauthorized grade changes, reports of possibly forged faculty signatures on grade rolls, lack of supervision and infrequent classes.

The former President of the NCAA, Myles Brand, worked diligently during his tenure to establish academic reform for intercollegiate athletics. Under Brand's leadership, the NCAA developed cutting-edge academic reform for intercollegiate athletics with its groundbreaking Academic Success Rate study in 2006. This was the first such study to be undertaken within the association, and it is unique in that it measures graduation outcomes for student-athletes. Now all three divisions have academic success rates that govern intercollegiate athletics. In addition to the academic success rate, student-athletes must make satisfactory progress towards graduation, this requires that all student-athletes must pass twelve credit hours each semester they are enrolled in school full time. To play, they must also maintain a 2.0 or better, according to the NCAA. It is important to note that some colleges and universities require that some student-athletes must maintain a GPA greater than a 2.0 to participate in intercollegiate athletics.

Many black student-athletes are taking just the bare minimum of credit courses needed to play. In the end, this decreases the likelihood of them completing their college education. Far too many black student-athletes will have used up all of their college eligibility and still need thirty or forty hours of course work to graduate. On many major university campuses athletics departments are taking unethical actions on behalf of the institutions to keep these athletes eligible from one season to the next. Graduation continues to be an afterthought, eligibility is the main emphasis. Another interesting factor that Powell raised was the ongoing assembly line of new young talented black athletes in virtually every urban community just waiting for their turn at bat to be the next big-time recruit to get played by intercollegiate athletics. With just a small window of opportunity for black athletes to make it professionally, the odds rarely favor them.

How many Dwyane Wades or LeBron James will actually make it to the big time? The world is full of former intercollegiate athletes who failed to complete college to capture that degree and also failed to obtain that professional contract for millions that they had been dreaming about since the fourth grade. We cannot forget about the few who defied the odds and made it to the professional ranks, leaving college early for the pros or staying all four years, have nothing to show for it in terms of a college degree, and are now have no money. Take, for example, Kenny Anderson, Scottie Pippin, Terrell Owens, to name just a few. There is yet another category of former intercollegiate athlete who has either turned to life of drugs and crime or is now working a low-wage hourly job and still daydreaming about past stardom. Even today there is a criminal element to intercollegiate athletics. It is truly criminal for these highly ethical and moral institutions of higher education to abuse and use the black student-athlete, but is the black student-athlete also must admit their guilt as well for just being stupid.

In an attempt to right a wrong, we must be completely open and honest with the black student-athlete about the realities of intercollegiate athletics. A serious effort must be made to deemphasize intercollegiate athletics to create a balance that places more emphasis on intercollegiate academics. Powell discussed another interesting point in his book: Too many black student-athletes are waiting for college to be that magic starting point in their academic and educational careers. They fail to realize that, at this point, it is nearly impossible to go back and gain the basic foundation of education in reading, writing, and arithmetic. During my freshman year in college in 1981, I wrote my very first college paper on the NCAA's Proposition 48, which proposed minimum high school grades and SAT scores for high school athletes to participate in intercollegiate athletics during their freshman year. This regulation was put into place as a safeguard for the students and intercollegiate athletics. It told high school principals and coaches that they must prepare these athletes in the classroom. Here we are now, some thirty years later still struggling with intercollegiate athletes' academic problems.

While researching various articles, I came across an insightful article about Kevin Ross article. Creighton University awarded Ross, a 6'-9" basketball player from Chicago a basketball scholarship. However, Kevin was not able to read above the second-grade level. He was allowed to play basketball for the school even though he could not read. After leaving school still not able to read, he eventually filed a law suit against the university, citing breach of contract in the late 1980s. According to Ross, the university recruited Ross even though he was "ill-equipped and unable to successfully participate" in the curriculum. In 1982, after he left Creighton, the twenty-three-year-old Kevin Ross would go on to enroll in Marva Collin's Westside Preparatory School in Chicago to learn how to read. He was then accepted at the Missouri Valley Conference although his entrance-exam scores were below the national average. He had a knee injury in his junior year and underwent surgery at the end of the season, during which his team won the conference title. His senior year was marked by dismal performances in athletics and the classroom. He averaged only three points a game. His team went 7–20. Despite tutoring and a course load that included classes in the theory of baseball and ceramics, Ross was placed on academic probation. At the end of what should have been his final school year, he was 1-1/2 years short in credits needed for graduation. I was truly amazed by Kevin Ross's story. To this day, I share his story with athletes I meet. Even today with all of the NCAA's major reform efforts, many cases resemble Kevin Ross's.

Fast forward to 2012, and yet another athlete's sad academic story. At the University of Memphis, Dasmine Cathey struggled from day one after landing on campus to pursue his dream of playing big-time college football. He was an outstanding high school athlete in Tennessee. He was a finalist for Tennessee Lineman of the Year in football and played on a state-championship basketball team at Ridgeway High in suburban Memphis, Tennessee. As a result of his stardom, he was given a pass. If not for football, and his hope of playing professionally, he never would have gone to college. His poor high-school grades and test scores forced him to sit out his first year at University of Memphis. To say that Cathey had an up-and-down academic and athletic career at the University of Memphis is an understatement. Dasmine Cathey kept his biggest secret from his teammates: He could not read. At night he would pull out a shoebox from under his bed with a set of First Grade, Level 1 reading books for ages 6 and 7. At the age of nineteen after completing high school and enrolling in college at the University of Memphis, he realized that he needed to learn how to read. Dasmine Cathey reported that he hated everything about school: reading, writing, and even the smell of books.

One of the biggest challenges facing college athletics today is the academic profile of black student-athletes. The University of Memphis has worked extremely hard to identify the increasing number of student-athletes who come to college severely ill prepared. This puts an extra burden on the university's athletic staff because the academic backgrounds of the football and basketball teams at the University of Memphis do not look like the rest of the student body population. Importantly, the student-athlete population has a higher graduation rate than that of the general population in many cases.

In contrast, Dasmine Cathey's academic path has been like a rollercoaster, his freshman year he had a 2.0. During his next semester Cathey's grade point average would fall to a 1.5. In one semester, he earned a astonishing 2.9 GPA, his highest during his college career while taking less challenging courses. During his last semester of his final season of football, Cathey failed three courses; his GPA fell below the 2.0 required to graduate. Now a senior and still dreaming about playing professional football, Cathey's GPA of .08 gave him a slim chance of graduating. Without the assistance of the University of Memphis athletic support staff, he would have not made it to this point.

The University of Memphis employs an eight-member academic team and twenty additional graduate assistants, interns, and tutors that support the university athletic department. They work hundreds of hours to ensure that their student-athletes can remain eligible according to the NCAA requirements. Under the new reform proposed by the NCAA, colleges and universities must provide evidence of academic support for student-athletes and students must show positive results or lose scholarships and postseason opportunities. Black athletes face a critical question: How can they perform at such a high level in athletic competition, and perform so poorly in the classroom.

Today black athletes are simply not comfortable in the college environment, and, truth be told, many have no interest in academics. Far too many black athletes continue to approach college for the wrong reasons, to prepare for a professional sports career, not to be professional citizens who work a normal 9-to-5 job. The NCAA has taken steps to promote professional careers after intercollegiate athletics. Throughout the media, we find various ads targeting intercollegiate athletes. One ad promises, "There are some 460,000 NCAA student-athletes, and just about all of them will be going pro in something other than sports." Theses spots can be seen on CBS, ESPN and CSTV. The ads range from serious to clever and even possibly humorous. However, at some point the black student-athlete need to understand that scoring in the classroom will bear better long-term opportunities beyond the football fields and basketball arena that are dominated by black athletes. They must also realize that, one day, their athletic skills are sure to decrease, through age or injury, and that there is always some new young buck waiting on the assembly line for his turn.

The problem is so pervasive at predominantly white colleges and universities that it is criminal. Data generated by the NCAA attempts to make the claim that black male student-athletes at Division I institutions graduate at higher rates than black men who do not play college sports. While this may be true across the entire Division I, it is not the case at the overwhelming majority of colleges and universities in the big conferences. In 2010, U.S. Secretary of Education, Arne Duncan, suggested that any sports team failing to graduate at least 40% of its players should be ineligible for participation in postseason play and championship contests. It appears that no one was listening to Secretary Duncan who played basketball himself in college at Harvard, but grew up playing street ball with disadvantaged black youth in Chicago's inner city. Many of Duncan's black playground buddies went on to Division I institutions, several failing to earn a college degree. It is critical for black student-athletes and their families that institutional leaders, the NCAA, and conference leaders pay more attention not only to overall team rates, but also racial trends and inequities. Racial inequities in academic progress should be given the same, if not tougher, standards by the NCAA. Take, for example, Ohio State University and Penn State University: Both received sanctions deeming them ineligible for postseason play in 2012 for nonacademic policy violations.

Black male student-athletes are often stereotyped as dumb jocks. One could easily summarize their status as blacks who attend college only to advance their sports careers and generate considerable revenue for the institution without learning much or seriously endeavoring to earn college degrees. Any effort to improve completion rates and academic success among black male student-athletes must include some emphasis on their confrontations with low expectations and stereotypes in classrooms and elsewhere on campus. At the institutional level, provosts, deans, and department chairs should engage faculty colleagues in substantive conversations and developmental exercises that raise consciousness about stereotypes and their racist and sexist assumptions about students of color and student-athletes in general.

If institutions are really serious about addressing the academic problems that continue to plague the black athlete, they must be willing to address the recruiting process. Coaches must revisit their recruiting methods related to black athletes. Coaches must not be allowed to do what they have done for years, recruit to win in the athletics arena at the expense of the academic arena. There is seemingly no true commitment to academic excellence when it comes to the black athlete at far too many public and private institutions where intercollegiate sports drive the institution's direction. This type of practice is truly reckless and should be unlawful to say the least. Presently, far too many of the nation's leading public and private institutions of higher education, including some HBCUs, continue to recruit and offer scholarships to black athletes who are academically unprepared and not the least bit motivated to perform beyond their athletic sport of choice. There is no question that the black athlete can be motivated to achieve academically, but only if more emphasis would be placed on the importance of academics by coaches, parents, and institutional leaders.

These academic and educational inequalities are particularly troublesome in terms of the overall plight of black male student-athletes in America. Each year more and more black student-athletes continue the underachiever cycle through their participation in intercollegiate athletics. This must change and it must change immediately. Don't believe the hype that black student-athletes are winning in big-time college sports and in the classroom. This is so troublesome because blacks are overrepresented in football and basketball. In terms of the academic race, blacks continue to fall short in their ability to earn a solid education let alone a college degree.

Consider for a moment the black male basketball and football players who enroll at one the major universities. They graduate from high school barely able to read and write a complete sentence. Purely because of the color of their skin and their athletic talents, they are awarded a college scholarship based on athletics. Truly, we are sending the wrong message to far too many young black athletes, their families, and the black community as a whole. When does the madness end in the academic exploitation of the black male student-athlete, or do we keep on keeping on because no one is really complaining or talking loudly. Helping all student-athletes graduate from college is the goal, but this is even more critical as it relates to the black male student-athlete. If these young men were not enrolled in college, there is very strong possibility that they may not or be accounted for at all. Or they may be a just another number in the prison–industrial complex that is also overpopulated by black males. We must not underestimate the extreme importance of educating and graduating the black male student-athletes and ensuring that they obtain a set of life skills that will ultimately ensure their survival beyond their sports days.

Importantly, less than 2% of college football players will earn the right to play professional football, and everyone knows that you cannot play forever. It is truly alarming that less than 50% of all black male student-athletes will not graduate within the allotted six years allowed by the U.S. Department of Education and the NCAA. Take, for example, the 2013 BCS National Football Champions, Florida State University, which posted a despicable 37% graduation rate for its black football players. Florida State University is only one of many institutions of higher education that underemphasizes academics compared to athletics. Only after the numbers went public did University President Eric Barron recommend that the athletic department hire academic tutors and advisors to improve its athletes' graduation rates.

Now, we must keep it real. These efforts are mainly for the black athletes, who, for the most part, were never actually prepared to handle the academic course load at the university level. They were athletic warriors that brought much attention and money to the university at the end of the day. The effort by Florida State University President was indeed a grand and bold one, but what took the university so long to spend the money and resources after years of continually exploiting young black male student-athletes?

Stanford University ranks as the top institution within the NCAA for graduating black football players at 82%. What is so amazing about Stanford is that it is also one of the nation's top-ranking academic institutions. Another factor about Stanford University is that they rank among the winningest intercollegiate programs. Another critical factor at Stanford is that the head football coach and the athletic director are both black, and huge advocates for academics. The university as a whole tends to place great emphasis and value on educational attainment. Other institutions with similar educational success with black student-athletes include Duke, Northwestern, and Vanderbilt University, which all seek to recruit student-athletes who have multiple college options. Student-athletes usually decide to attend Stanford, Duke, or Northwestern for the outstanding academic track record, not the outstanding winning percentage and national television exposure.

More coaches, athletics administrators, and institutional leaders must place more importance on academics. It is unfortunate that schools like Florida State, Oklahoma, and other public institutions have paid so little attention to what Stanford and Duke are doing in academics with their black male student-athletes. There is no question that at Stanford and Duke, these gifted and talented black male student-athletes need less help to balance and juggle their academic studies and devote the time needed to be outstanding athletes in their chosen sports. However, these two institutions are committed to ensuring that the student-athletes are successful both academically and athletically. More efforts must be made to publicly embarrass any institution that fails to graduate the black student-athlete within the six-year window. There must be more accountability; if they are willing to admit and accept underprepared black student-athletes, they cannot afford not to identify ways to improve their ability to read and write and prepare them to graduate at some point even if it takes more than the NCAA's six years.

For the most part, we all know that athletics is often viewed as a way into many of these institutions for some students. However, far too many traditionally white institutions and some HBCUs continue to place far too much emphasis on winning in athletics, encouraging the black male athlete to make a choice between academics and athletics. The issue of academic scandals in intercollegiate athletics continues to plague many of our finest publicly funded institutions. Academic scandals or academic fouls, however one would like to call it; at the end of the day, it still smells bad. As long as these institutions with these storied and rich academic histories continue to admit black male student-athletes who are not academically prepared for the serious rigor of the academic challenges, we are sure to witness more academic fouls and flags for these institutions.

One of the most notable and storied academic institutions within the contexts of the NCAA and the nation in general is the University of North Carolina at Chapel Hill. The Tar Heel nation was rocked first by allegations of an academic scandal connecting several black football players and the African and Afro-American Studies Department to academic fraud. The university proudly graduates 74% of its black male student-athletes. But the critical question should be, with what type of degree and how successful are these graduates in the real world? The NCAA does a decent job tracking the graduation rates, but with little attention on the types of majors and the specific degrees being awarded to black male student-athletes.

After the scandal at UNC went public, thanks to the *New York Times,* a grand jury moved forward and charged a former professor at the university with fraudulently accepting payment to teach a class where black athletes frequently enroll. Within the context of this made-up class, there was no homework, no tests or exams, and virtually no faculty oversight. Members of the grand jury believed that this class was created solely for the purpose helping several black members of the university football team earn credits during the summer needed to retain their eligibility. The New York Times reported that there was no way that the UNC faculty member could have acted independently to develop and offer such a fraudulent class without others within the university knowing about it.

On the heels of the 2010 football scandal at UNC Chapel Hill, yet another academic scandal challenged the university's academic integrity in 2014. This time it involved former UNC basketball star and former NBA player Rashad McCants in an interview with ESPN's "Outside the Lines." According to McCants, while he was a student-athlete at UNC he had tutors who actually wrote his papers for his classes. During the interview, McCants stated that he thought that having someone to do your work was just a part of the college experience for star players. During his stay at the university, McCants helped UNC win the 2005 NCAA championship before leaving college after his junior year to join the NBA for a short tour. McCants is yet another sad story: The star player preforms so well athletically, but after his college career ends, he has nothing to fall back on. McCants states he was just at UNC to play basketball and win games, he had no idea that he needed to go to class or do college work; that was why he had tutors. Of course head basketball coach Roy Williams disagrees with the McCants' statements concerning the university and the athletic-department officials' interest or lack of interest in the overall welfare of its black student-athletes.

The allegations levied against the university during this time stemmed from a completely separate NCAA investigation involving the football team which resulted in several black players being suspended and the coach being fired. The NCAA investigation found that there was improper conduct between black football players and the African and Afro-American Studies department, where the NCAA discovered that a majority of the black athletes on the football team had taken and were currently taking classes. They had been receiving favorable grades from this department for several years. This raised major suspicion, thus resulting in the NCAA looking deeper into the ethical behavior surrounding the university and student-athlete academic affairs. The NCAA uncovered that for years black athletes in both football and basketball, the two top revenue-generating sports for the university, had been offered courses that may or may not have met. Many of these courses had very little structure or little to no requirements, such as one research paper at the end of the semester. Some courses were established as independent study courses. Surely, university officials knew what was going on with the black student-athletes.

During the NCAA investigation, Mary Willingham a former learning specialist hired to work with the black student-athletes at UNC indicated that for the most part all of the independent courses were designed to help keep the black student-athletes eligible despite the limited academic readiness of the majority of the black student-athletes. At UNC, the NCAA investigation also uncovered unauthorized grade changes and even forged signatures on grade rosters. Now, it is important to note that UNC is not the only large public institutions to get caught and they won't be the last to be embarrassed in the public for academic misconduct. In a similar case at Auburn University in 2006, the Sociology department was found guilty of awarding favorable grades to student-athletes on the university's football team. The NCAA stepped in and immediately placed the university on probation. We must all pay more attention to the departments where the majority of the black student-athletes study and challenge the athletic administration as to why are so many black student-athletes being directed to major in courses such as black studies, criminal justice, sports management, sociology, hotel management and liberal studies. We must also begin the critical discussion about what black student-athletes, with limited academic skills in the beginning, can do with a degree that they really did not properly earn when it is time to put that college degree to work.

CHAPTER SIX

Reevaluating the Crisis of Black-Athletes After Edwards and Rhoden

"Champions aren't made in gyms. Champions are made from something they have deep inside them—a desire, a dream, a vision. They have to have last-minute stamina, they have to be a little faster, they have to have the skill and the will. But the will must be stronger than the skill."

—Muhammad Ali

The Edwards Perspective

Scholar and historian Harry Edwards was a student-athlete at San Jose State University during the 1960s. Upon graduating with honors, Edwards was approached by the National Football League as a prospect for the NFL Draft. However, Edwards decided to pursue a graduate degree in sociology rather than enter the draft. Edwards attended Cornell University for both his M.A. and Ph.D. degrees in sociology. He has published two books: *The Revolt of the Black Athlete* and *Black Students,* twenty-eight articles, and his dissertation, *The Sociology of Sport.* Edwards eventually joined the NFL and won four Super Bowl rings during his professional career.

Some years ago, scholar and historian Harry Edwards noted the central roots that continue to disable the black athlete today. According to Edwards, black families are often too eager to gamble the lives of their children by pushing them toward a career in sports very early on, neglecting other important personal and cultural investments. Edwards further noted that one prime vehicle of self-realization, and the path to social and economic advancement, is academic excellence. According to Edwards, this has created a serious crisis not only for the black athlete, but black society as a whole. Edwards noted other critical issues that must be taken into account: First, the race-based presumption is that blacks are athletically superior and intellectually inferior. Second, media propaganda has skillfully painted black athletics as the quickest and most accessible route to social mobility. Third, Edwards noted the continued lack of credible and visible black role models outside of sports.

Overwhelmingly, black athletes continue to pursue a career in sports at any cost. Black athletes must be informed that there are more options in sports than just being the athlete. We must redirect them to other career options in the sports arena such as administration and management. The circumstances surrounding this crisis for black athletes has become an institutional problem for blacks. The academic underdevelopment of black athletes further suggests a crisis in the black athletes' overall development.

Fewer and fewer blacks are moving into professional careers such as medicine, law, education, science, engineering, and politics. Far too many blacks are willing to gamble on making it in sports at the expense of developing their talent in the classroom. Another important issue Edwards raised is that far too many young blacks have become victims to the social conditions within their communities. Because of increasing social problems, many blacks between sixteen and twenty-nine years of age have been taken out of the game by their involvement with the U.S. legal system. With nearly one quarter of all black males sixteen to twenty-nine under the control of the court system, at least one quarter of black professional potential is threatened as well. It is important to note that the high incarceration and dropout rates that continue to plague black men have significantly influenced the underdevelopment of black athletes and black institutions as a whole.

With few obvious alternatives, an increasing percentage of black athletes have marginalized themselves into becoming the next sport superstar. Therefore, all of their effort, time, and commitment are placed on making it in sports, especially basketball and football. The overall societal issues further suggest that academically and socially underdeveloped black athletes are unable to compete with other blacks and nonblacks in the real world. Finally, Edwards notes that the overall key to resolving the crisis for black athletes centers around the overall involvement and active participation of black institutions. According to Edwards, young blacks critically need the development of black social institutions, starting with the family.

The development of positive opportunities within the various black institutions is what black youth lack. We must fully acknowledge and accept that the lack of positive black institutional influences seriously threatens black athletes. Sports participation cannot continue to be an obsession or preoccupation for the undeveloped black athlete. It is important to note that both intercollegiate and professional sports operations are similar to that of the operation of a slave plantation. Athletes are required to use their skills and talents. At the end of the day it is all about the economic benefit for the institutions. There are the cheering fans, including owners, college president, and even board members encouraging athletes to perform their best under sometimes stressful conditions. Some may argue that, at the professional level, these athletes are getting paid, so they cannot actually be slaves. Even at the college level, they are receiving scholarships, so many are quick to argue that this is not slavery, it is a volunteer action on the athlete's part.

The Rhoden Perspective

William C. Rhoden has been writing about sports for the *New York Times* since March 1983. Previously, he was a copy editor in the Sunday Week in Review section from October 1981, when he joined the newspaper. Before joining the *Times,* Mr. Rhoden spent more than three years with the *Baltimore Sun* as a columnist. Before that, he was associate editor of *Ebony* magazine from 1974 to 1978. He attended Morgan State University in Baltimore and, while there, acted as assistant sports information director.

According to William Rhoden, the key factors are, and always have, been revenue generation at the expense of black athletes. He further states that black-athletes are the oil that runs the economic engines for a number of professional and intercollegiate sports teams. The key to understanding the plantation reference is that there is no shared power among the players and owners on the professional or collegiate level. At the professional level, the athlete can be brought, traded, and or discarded at will. There are too many stories to tell about black athletes seemingly moving from one plantation to the next.

According to Rhoden, the true challenge for black athletes in the twenty-first century is to make good on their athletes' potentials with limited resources. The underdeveloped black athlete with limited resources is less likely to be in control and more likely to be controlled. Rhoden believes that black athletes will take to that conveyor belt and willingly accept the plantation power structure. One of the major challenges that continues' to confront black athletes, Rhoden noted, was the overwhelming lack of understanding about how to deal effectively with the "Black Power" of black athletes in the world of the "White Controlled Power" structure of the NCAA and professional sports. At the intercollegiate level at many predominantly white institutions and in the professional ranks, the CEOs, owners, and coaches, the majority of whom are white, continue to get richer on the backs of black athletes. It is sad how the black community continues to pimp some of its brightest and most gifted talents for greener opportunities, but the underdeveloped black communities remain the same year after year. Black communities continue to lack the most basic of resources (education, nutrition, health care, crime prevention, and poverty relief) in this twenty-first century United States of America, where all the world looks in terms of human and civil rights.

Continuing the plantation analogy, many black athletes have been able to escape the ghetto plantations of the projects to the NCAA for intercollegiate preparation and a chance to perform at the highest level, the "professional ranks," as a safe haven. Again we must understand the role of the ghetto plantation in advancing the underdevelopment of black-athletes and blacks in general. Similar to the plantation, ghetto plantation residents are constantly being monitored by the police under the guise of safety. They are monitored to keep them in order and in their place. They have limited resources and limited access to quality education, proper nutrition, healthy food, quality healthcare, and safe communities.

As you can see, escaping from the ghetto plantation can be a real psychological challenge for black athletes. They may think that they have successfully run away from its conditions when they arrive in big-time sports. However, they frequently return home to visit family and friends who remain trapped in the modern-day equivalent of the plantation and slavery. Columnist and author William Rhoden's analysis in *Forty Million Dollar Slaves* is incredible and very timely. This book is my attempt to add my two cents to Rhoden's remarkable narrative of the black athlete both past and present.

One must completely consider several reasons why NCAA football and basketball players with amateur status are also nothing less than slaves. The *Atlanta Black Star,* which was created to provide empowering narratives for all people of African descent and everyone who shares our culture, provides several vital points explaining why the NCAA and its member institutions can easily be discussed as an extension of the slave plantation. First, consider how colleges and universities recruit and acquire the black student-athlete, who will ultimately work towards their debts tirelessly without any pay. Yes, they may receive scholarships or a form of grant-in-aid, but there is no real compensation for their slave like tireless efforts. If the athlete does not receive an education as a result of the scholarship, the scholarship is worthless. If the athlete is not able to rise up and find a better life, his time spent in college is wasted. Consider for a moment that NCAA college sports generate upwards of $8 billion annually from combined television rights, ticket sales, and licensing fees. At the heart of this billion-dollar industry is the exploitation of young black male labor at the amateur-athlete level.

It is important to note that only in the United States have the NCAA and its member institutions have an effective amateur labor market whereby black student-athletes are recruited, acquired, and managed mainly by nonblack coaches and administrators. In particular, black males continue to outnumber white males on NCAA football and basketball teams. Once black student-athletes are acquired by the various NCAA colleges and universities, for two to four years their talent is locked into the collegiate labor pool by their athletic scholarship. An athletic scholarship is nothing less than a contract agreement between the NCAA member institutions and the student-athlete. The colleges and universities retain sole rights as did the slave owners. Institutions continue to benefit from unlimited future potential earning through television rights, ticket sales, and licensing fees, all based on the free labor of black student-athletes. Within the context of the scholarship/contract, the student-athlete is prohibited by the NCAA from benefiting financially in any form from his talent, despite the money he helps colleges and universities earn. Does this not sound like some of the same forms of slavery imposed by whites on blacks.

Take, for example, the 2014 case of former UCLA basketball star Ed O'Bannon, who sued the NCAA and the video-gaming industry for the use of his likeness in a video game years after he left the institution. As another example, consider Jadeveon Clowney, who was the first player auctioned in the 2014 NFL draft. From 2011, the University of South Carolina Gamecocks benefited greatly from ticket sales and the sale of Clowney's jersey, not to mention the television deals for the Southeastern Athletic Conference, all based on his labor on Saturday afternoons.

The NCAA cannot entirely prevent the student-athlete from earning money for their likeness or for signing jerseys, game booklets, and other sports-related merchandise, but, based on the scholarship/contract's structure, the NCAA can prohibit the student-athlete from receiving any financial profits that would jeopardize their amateur status. If a student-athlete does receives any financial profits for engaging in any of the above mentioned activities, he or she is subject to severe sanctions and penalties imposed by the NCAA and its member institutions. Furthermore, such student-athletes may jeopardize their eligibility to continue their college careers under the current NCAA guidelines and rules.

At the end of the day, the NCAA and its member institutions completely own all of the rights to the student-athlete in perpetuity from the date they are acquired and have signed that scholarship/contract. This agreement affords both the NCAA and its member institutions the ability to legally gain valuable financial profits from the student-athletes' free labor in sporting competition and related activities, including college product endorsements, ticket sales, and merchandise licensing. In fact, the NCAA and intercollegiate athletics is the only game in the world where young blacks classified as amateurs can generate billions of dollars for the controlling organizations. Another important fact is that the NCAA is the only organized body of amateur sports that has the power to control and manage young black student-athletes while earning huge financial profits largely on the backs, legs, and arms of an amateur black labor force between eighteen and twenty-two years of age.

Despite being awarded a sports scholarship to attend college, if a student-athlete is injured during his college career, there is a strong chance he will not finish college. Another factor is that, in most cases, the final decision of whether to, first, cover the medical expenses and, second, honor the student-athlete's scholarship is often made by the institution athletic department. Very few NCAA institutions provide the student-athlete with a guaranteed scholarship/contact for the full college career. Even more troublesome is the issue of potential long-term psychological effects directly related to sports injuries sustained during the student-athlete's tenure. At present, nothing on the books speaks to providing any form of healthcare coverage or health insurance for the student-athletes after their college-playing career has ended. Each year, countless student-athletes sustain head injuries, broken limbs, memory loss, and other injuries that are sure to produce psychological impairments.

Let us not forget that black slaves also receive no pay for their relentless labor, and certainly no short-term or long term healthcare benefits, yet they produced large profits for the white slave owner. Both slave and student-athlete are granted room and board for their service. Yes, things have changed somewhat for the student-athlete today, but not necessarily for the better. The student-athletes today are likely to receive a solid handshake, a pat on the back, and sometimes a word of comfort from white coaches, boosters, and fans for their efforts. They are also afforded the opportunity to play in big televised games before millions of adoring fans, and they might receive an oversized championship ring or trophy valued at less than $1000. Meanwhile, the NCAA and its member institutions are running to the bank to cash in on their legal exploitation tactics involving the black student-athlete.

Another important factor about the college athletic scholarship/ contract is that, similar to the plantation owners, the coaches have the authority to fulfill or dash the dreams and aspirations of young black athletes. Yes, student-athletes do have the right to appeal should their scholarship be rescinded. But, in most cases, the coach and athletic director will have the final say on whether to honor it. Importantly, the NCAA continues to prohibit student-athletes from working during their student-athletic career. They are not allowed to earn any form of money while on a scholarship/contract. The only exception is earning money to help with their college-related expenses. Unfortunately, the majority of black student-athletes come from very poor and underdeveloped communities with limited resources and poor educational systems. Furthermore, there are very few employment opportunities for black athletes lacking the developmental and cultural skills needed to survive beyond athletics. Sadly, football, basketball, rapping, and selling drugs have become the quickest way for upward mobility for the young black male nonprofessional.

As I revisited William Rhoden's *Forty Million Dollar Slaves* in 2014 while preparing to write this book, the remarks of former Los Angeles Clippers owner Donald Sterling provided yet another disturbing example of the negative side of race in sports that further supports Rhoden's claim. Here again, Rhoden does an excellent job of enlightening the reader on the rise, fall and redemption of the black athlete. During Donald Sterling's tenure as owner of the NBA's Los Angeles Clippers, he proved to be a master overseer and played a significant role in acquiring, trading, and owning high-priced black athletes. Sterling was also of the mindset that, as the owner, he had the right and obligation to treat them as he felt necessary. Even more alarming, although Sterling brought the team for almost nothing, Sterling has made significant financial profits from his black athletic labor force in terms of ticket sales, merchandising, product endorsements, and licensing fees. In 2013, Sterling was caught on tape telling his then half-black girl friend that he did not like the that fact that she hangs around blacks and that they were not welcome to his "Games." Nearly every basketball player on the Los Angeles Clippers is black. In fact, even the head coach, Doc Rivers, was black. He gained an enormous profit when forced to sell in 2014 for his racist remarks about blacks.

Sterling's actions further support Rhoden's theory that helps us all better conceptualize this new plantation system we call organized professional sports, whereby a few young black athletes are getting rich, while the white owners are getting insanely wealthy on the old plantation slavery system that was well defined and engineered by the good old boys of yesteryear. Sterling and other professional owners are seemingly allowed to continue this deep-rooted historical racism in an overt system of slavery. Despite the financial profits afforded to a few young blacks, those who play football and basketball have become slaves to their respective sports. The sad part about this is that, if not for these sporting opportunities, there is no telling where these young men would end up.

Rhoden clearly demonstrates the connection between professional sports and the old slave system by reestablishing the long-standing history of white power and control in both professional and intercollegiate sports where blacks are consistently exploited for huge financial profits. Throughout the history of organized sports, blacks have been allowed to participate, but, by and large, whites have historically been the biggest winners. To date, only two blacks have held a majority ownership in the modern sports world, Robert Bob Johnson and Michael Jordan. In 2010, Johnson sold his controlling interest to Jordan, making him the only black majority owner of a professional men's sports team.

Rhoden was clearly trying to convey that professional and even college sports, wherein black athletes are the centerpiece of the attraction, are nothing less than the new slave plantations with such upgraded amenities as giant jumbo screens, luxury boxes, and extra entertainment on top of the main attraction, the black superstar slaves acquired to attract white consumers. It is even more troublesome that that attitude of white owners, coaches, managers, and even the fans is to care and provide for their young black slave stars until they misbehave, lose a step or two, or become less competitive.

It is important understand that Rhoden's depiction of professional and college sports teams as new-generation slave plantations with new forms of technological amenities have raised the stakes in the sports world with regard to race. The overall attitude of whites associated with sports is seemingly to take care or provide their prized young black boys and junior men until they lose their value. It is unfortunate that so many white coaches and managers share Donald Sterling's attitudes and values about blacks, they only seem to care about their prized black athletes as long as they continue to add to the owner's wealth. Rhoden suggests that black athletes have failed to see how they are being exploited and used by the system all in the name of making a profit for the owners, colleges, and universities.

Rhoden suggests that black athletes have failed to see how they are being exploited and used by the system to make a profit for the owners, colleges, and universities. He provides an excellent illustration of black sports history, with detailed narratives focused on the actual stories of successful and not-so-successful black athletes during a period of white-dominated racist power structure when many blacks were denied the opportunity to participate with or against white athletes. Rhoden then argues brilliantly that integration posed relatively few problems for the white sports world and fans in general because over time white institutions and organizations quickly gained access to a pool of cheap, young, black athletic talent, thus allowing white coaches, owners, managers, trainers, accountants, lawyers and even secretaries the opportunity to gain financially from their new slaves' on-the-field and -court talents.

According to Rhoden and as with slavery, it is at this point that most black athletes may have lost their way in terms of their connection to self and their ability to become a part of their expanding worlds as sports figures. Suddenly, young black athletes found themselves in the middle of a constant struggle Rhoden represents as a lost tribe of African ancestors. Rhoden describes the young black athletes as someone adrift in a new white world of sports where white coaches, fans, boosters, agents, team owners, and network executives all profit from the talents and skills of black athletes. Rhoden's historical narrative also identifies what he calls the jockey syndrome using the exceptional story of Isaac Murphy, the most prominent and wealthiest black jockey of the nineteenth century.

During Murphy's brilliant career, he won three Kentucky Derby races and even employed a white valet during the racing season. Murphy earned between $15,000 and $20,000 dollars per year at the height of his career. However, all was not always good for Murphy and his career. He faced unprecedented pressures from white jockeys and the white racing world in general. He was forced out of horse racing by his white opponents in the end. As whites control the horse-racing industry, they finally had their way through intense forms of physical interference with the black jockeys, both on the track and off. In the end, the white jockeys were able to achieve what they had set out to do, deny black jockeys the opportunity to complete in horse racing. Rhoden also provides a grand account of the first black major-league baseball player, Fleetwood Walker, as he battled the racist white sports world before the days of the National Baseball League (NBL).

Rhoden also describes the racist attitudes of powerful white figures in the United States government who pursued and destroyed black heavyweight boxing champion Jack Johnson. The United States government and the boxing industry were not at peace with Johnson's parading around with white women, breaking the rules and taboos established by the powerful white men who controlled the world. Johnson was a robust black man who made a living punishing men in the boxing ring, in most cases white men. They finally got their way when he lost his boxing title for being jailed several times by the white establishment on ridiculous charges of Mann Act violations. Rhoden also briefly discusses Muhammad Ali's similar racial struggles with the U.S. injustice system, including both victories and defeats connected to racial disharmony between blacks and whites in the world of sports.

Under the Negro Baseball League system, black superstar players could only play against other black players before Jackie Robinson broke the color barrier to play in what we now call the National Baseball League. Leading up to Jackie Robinson, Rhoden provides a detailed account of black baseball pioneer Rudy Foster, who organized and ran the Negro Baseball League. Foster literally suffered mentally and eventually died believing he had failed to accomplish what he perceived as true baseball integration: having the Negro Baseball League complete against the all-white National Baseball League. Foster wanted the Negro Baseball League to become a central part of the National Baseball League, not as a supplier of black players, but as a complete franchise. Foster put so much energy into this concept that he eventually suffered a mental breakdown in 1926 and died shortly thereafter.

The mental breakdown was believed to be induced by the white baseball's refusal to allow negro teams to join the National Baseball League. For years after Foster died, black baseball players suffered a critical vacuum in overall vision and leadership, and the Negro Baseball League eventually faded into oblivion. Rhoden carefully describes how white sporting institutions and white powerbrokers continue even today to make significant financial gains and profits from the skills and talents of young black-athletes: the high school pike line or what Rhoden describes as the conveyor-belt theory. Rhoden's narrative about the conveyor-belt theory is a brilliant analysis of a successful system whereby underemployed black males from poor communities are being herded in droves to white colleges and universities. There, they are being exploited by an educational and sporting system that is seemingly uninterested in educating poor black males and only interested in developing their athletic talents and skills which will more often than not result in more financial gains and profits for the system than for the players.

According to Rhoden, the conveyor-belt theory emphasizes individual success, not the system that continues to exploit the black athlete by distributing power unequally: Professional basketball and football are still largely controlled by whites, but nearly three quarters of the players are black. As with the old plantations, the success of the whites who run the show ultimately depends on the efforts and labor of their black athletes. These athletes are nothing less than a new generation of slaves who are being paid millions in some cases, as long as they do not make too much noise or embarrass white folks and object to being managed, coached, and controlled in a racist sport industry.

Moving away from Rhoden for a moment, we must also consider what the group members from the Last Poets said in 1970. "Niggers play football, baseball and basketball while the white man cuttin' off their balls … Niggers tell you they're ready to be liberated, but when you say 'let's take our liberation.'" However, in the end niggers will reply all too often, "I was just playin'." For so many young black athletes in today's modern game all of the emphasis is on developing capitalist money-making opportunities, whereby white coaches and owners with some assistance from blacks who have learned the same mentality of directing the black superstar to white athletic handlers or overseers. They operate like leeches on these young black male athletes who are most likely uneducated. Their main emphasis is to suck or drain all of the possible juice out the black athlete like a fresh fruit ready from the market. Even at the college level, there is truly something seriously broken with American athletic. It is nothing less than a modern-day slave trade, a form of legal slavery or pimping that continues to psychologically shatter the lives of the far too many young black male athletes.

Psychologically, everything has deep roots for black athletes in today's NFL and NBA drafts, or, as some call them, the "Athletic Salve Auctions." To properly understand how sports evolved, all one needs to do is examine how the sporting industry first realized that there were huge profits associated with the physical and psychological exploitation of young black athletes. After the African slaves were first colonized by whites, there was a real need to identify a new group to be exploited. The black community, with its troublesome ills and increasingly limited opportunities for upward mobility offered just such a target. Over the years, more and more attention has been given to the poor black communities that continue to produce the new "black product" such as Desmond "Dez" Bryant, Adrian Peterson, and Cam Newton. I have nothing but respect for these young men for their accomplishments, but the game was changed for entirety by the introduction of black athletes to white sports.

The white sports world continues to look to the black athletes, thus allowing the athletes to release their built up aggression though sports while maintaining the whites' control. Before the emergence of modern big-time sports, black sporting events were barbarous, even including lion fighting. Whites were quick to realize that blacks were quicker, more agile, could jump higher, run faster, and were more spontaneous than white when it came to sports. Therefore, white slave owners began to create sporting events and venues that featured blacks as the centerpiece. In today's sports world, very little has changed since plantation slavery.

From examining the history of black athletes and athletic competition involving blacks, it appears that whites continue to view black athletes through the lens of profits. The truth of the matter is that, similar to black slaves, black athletes have never been viewed as more than an object or tool to amass huge profits. The mental, physical, and even spiritual makeup of black athletes are why whites are so fascinated and somewhat tolerant of the black athlete's behaviors.

Whites understand today and understood in the slave days the need to acquire and control this black product. The key for the whites who remain most interested in the young black product is to, by any means necessary, reprogram the black athlete's mentality to ensure that they remain unliberated. In order words, blacks can only be as good as the white-controlled athletic organization structure will allow them to be. Understanding the true value of the black athlete requires first and foremost for black athletes to value themselves completely. Without understanding their value as human beings in general, they will only lose value over time, and the black product will ultimately lose its profit potential. This is true for both the college and the professional ranks.

Therefore, examining the Atlantic slave trade involves connecting the slaves of the past to the new world of sporting slavery. The NFL and NBA auctions or drafts, depending on who is watching, are similar to the slave auctions. In training camps conducted by various NFL and NBA teams prior to the auction night, prized young black studs are showcased and tested in fancy high tech stadiums and arenas so white and black coaches, general managers, and team owners can evaluate the skills and talents of the black athletes. The athletes are then graded, which will ultimately determine the financial worth of the black athlete. During this period, team officials carefully evaluate the black athletes in a variety of ways, including their attitudes, values, physical strength, ability, and agility. Once the data has been collected and analyzed, the athletes that best meet the needs of the team are those who will attract fans and drive organizational profits. With the testing complete, the names of the best black athletes are then passed on to the white team executives and team owners as in the days of the old-school plantation. Then, the final acquisition occurs in front of millions in the form of a televised auction. As during the heyday of the slave trade, emphasis is on the black athletes' height, weight, overall size, speed, and strength.

According to the National Football League's Players Association, the average career for a NFL player is only 3.5 years, and the average annual salary was only $770,000 in 2009. In the NBA, players' careers average only 4.7 years, and they will earn on average $5.84 million over their career. It is equally important to note that the NFL employs three times as many players as the NBA. In 2009, there were 1,696 NFL players, compared to only 435 NBA players. Black representation in the NFL in 2009 was 78%, while blacks made up about 80% of the NBA.

Another concern is the psychological trap that continues to catch many black athletes. They are quick to hire white sports agents to negotiate their contacts and to also handle much of the financial affairs. This often also involves interactions with other white businessmen who do not value the world from which these young black athletes come. These white agents often end up representing their black client on one hand, while largely dealing with other white owners and general managers with similar backgrounds and prejudices about blacks in general.

This begs the question: Who are the sports agents really working for? Language use is another troublesome factor to consider as it relates to the white sports agent marketing the black athlete to white owners: Listen to how they describe the overall size, height, weight, speed, and abilities of their athletes before the annual NFL and NBA auction or draft. This reminds us all yet again that this is just another form of slave trade, not a celebrated draft selection show as it is presented to the general public. The only minor difference is that some of today's black athletes are paid millions for their services. However, at the end of the day the black athletes, continue to earn pennies compared to what the owners and the majority of white executives earn in general. Annually, the white owners are racking up billions in profits. Comedian Chris Rock said it well in his stand-up act about the Shaquille O'Neil. According to Rock, Shaquille is rich, but the man who writes Shaquille's check is a wealthy white man. Long after a player's career ends, the teams and owners are still more valuable and continue to collect billions annually.

The NFL was established in 1920, nearly one hundred years ago. The NBA was established 1946 and just celebrated its seventieth birthday. By all standards, black athletes today are in worse shape psychologically than any other time in the history of organized sports, despite the money they earn. They are less likely to be educated and liberated mentally in their thinking about their white-controlled and managed industry. What is also alarming and troublesome is how slavery has taken shape in the form of amateur sports. In general, black athletes have collectively earned upwards of billions of dollars, but they have very little to show for it with the exception of a bunch of receipts goods sold to them by nonblacks. Except for a small handful of black athletes, most do not even support black community charities and black communities from which they come. Furthermore, with all of their newfound riches, they lack the knowledge and education necessary to open businesses and make investments in their black communities to improve the future of the youngest of our black citizens who arc subject to dead-end lives in poverty-stricken black communities. Today, there are more black millionaire sports figures than at any other time in the history of professional sports. However, blacks as a whole are still larger consumers than producers.

Another critical factor to consider about most black athletes who hire white agents is that these white agents do a great job keeping black athletes far away from the black community that supported and nourished them during their lowest moments in life when they had so little. Thanks to the concerted efforts of the white agents, black athletes are more likely to donate large amounts of money and time to white charities such as the

United Way and other white-managed charities than to local black church- and community-related charities. They are also more likely to make public appearances with white charitable organizations and little white kids than with poor black kids from their own poor black communities.

It is important to note that white sports agents, just like white coaches and owners are not at all interested in the business of liberating the black athlete economically, socially, or spiritually. They are all mainly interested in making money from their association with the black athlete. The white sports agents, along with other white managers help to enforce unspoken and explicit codes that encourage the athlete to avoid rocking the boat, to make nice and not jeopardize their lucrative perks. The true root of the problem with the black athlete is the threat that engaging in causes and issues that management might consider politically unsavory would lead to a lower earnings potential.

The roles our public high schools and colleges play in the psychological destruction of the black athlete cannot be ignored. Before they enter the professional ranks, high schools and colleges have established a solid foundation of exploiting and pimping of the youngest of the black athletic pool, and no one in the black community seems alarmed at all. Our schools are at the center of the food chain as they keep the supply of young black talent moving to and through college on the hope of being the next professional star to sign that multimillion-dollar contact. As high school programs continue to provide colleges and university programs with black athletes, colleges collect millions in revenue from the use and exposure of amateur athletes. The key is to track the money associated with intercollegiate athletics: Such institutions as Notre Dame, Alabama, North Carolina, and UCLA will profit handsomely from their athletic programs.

How often do we continue to observe college-related merchandise for sale that is unrelated to athletics? The answer is, "Not very often." When you see UNC or Notre Dame gear, it is usually sports related: tee-shirts, hats, socks, jackets, watches, posters, and more. No one is marketing academic gear for sale. Not if they want to make huge profits at the end of the day. It is the athletic items that everyone wants. This money goes directly to the university account, not the student-athletes' accounts. Another significant factor to consider is the local and state economic impact as result of the athletic activities associated with the colleges and universities. The money keeps flowing to these colleges and universities, thus funding new huge construction projects and buildings, creating new jobs, and recycling money in the hands of large white contractors with little to no interest in the improving the black communities or the lives of those who reside in them.

The Other Side of Business Related to Big-Time College Athletics

The opportunities for black contractors to land lucrative construction contracts are slim to none. It is damn near impossible for the black contractor to obtain a piece of the contract as a subcontractor. The good-old-boy system continues the process of keeping money segregated, which is largely generated on the backs of the black athletes through their free labor. A prime example is the University of South Carolina's overall local economy. Total economic impact of USC football in the local region of Columbia South Carolina exceeded $6 million per game from 2012 to 2014. When you combine the Clemson and University of South Carolina athletic programs, the state of South Carolina receives a tremulous economic boost from black participation in sports. The overall economic impact from these universities in the state of South Carolina exceeds $100 million annually. Upwards of 90% of the contract dollars are awarded to white contractors, many of whom have close ties to the university. Dr. Lonnie Randolph, the State President for the South Carolina NAACP has been championing the fight for black businesses seeking to do work with the University of South Carolina. He has been demanding that things change to give black contractors the same opportunities that white contractors have been afforded for hundreds of years. Randolph, who just happens to be prominent optometrist, clearly can see that the poor black and white citizens of South Carolina deserve better. That is why he is viewed by many as the real public defender for the voiceless. According to Dr. Randolph, white contractors continue to benefit through the good-old-boy system from the proceeds flowing to the university system from exploiting and pimping the black athlete for their free labor.

The exploitation of college athletes can be further explained by examining ESPN's *30 for 30* documentary entitled "The Fab Five," which aired in March of 2011. Former University of Michigan star Chris Webber openly stated during the documentary how Michigan made millions of dollars by the selling of his Number 4 jersey during his tenure at the university and that he received nothing from the university except the opportunity to run up and down the court while thousands of fans cheered. Similar to Chris Webber, Jadeveon Clowney of the University of South Carolina was the 2014 number-one overall NFL selected player. Clowney, also greatly helped the university rake in an unprecedented amount of money through the sale of his Number 7 jersey. According to Webber, during his Michigan days, even the shoe giant Nike got in on the exploitation game: Michigan made huge profits from Webber's stardom.

Webber's teammate and now NBA color analyst Jalen Rose also shared during the 30 for 30 documentary that Nike cashed in on the Michigan basketball team's long baggie shorts and black socks that revolutionized the college basketball game from short shorts and traditional white socks. This concept generated, and continues to generate millions of dollars for Nike and those associated with Nike: athletic conferences, coaches, and even athletic directors. It is important to note that at many universities, such as Georgetown, UNC, Michigan, and Michigan State, coaches are entitled to and have structured contacts with such athletic-shoe companies as Nike, Reebok, and Adidas. They can earn upwards of one million dollars annually, while the black athlete is left in the dark wishing and hoping.

Anyone, who follows the NCAA and March Madness know it is a multibillion-dollar event built around amateur sports. The lucrative television and video deals allow many people to make a great deal of money via amateur sports. At the end of the day, the wealth extraction from the black community alone by the NCAA and its member institutions exceeds one billion dollars annually. Author, political analyst, and social commentator, Dr. Boyce D. Watkins suggests that some of the money being generated by the NCAA could and should work its way back to the black community where it could improve the failing schools, black unemployment, and urban violence that continue to plague poor black communities. Watkins is a leading black scholars' known for his educational and social justice advocacy work. He has also been outspoken about the right or lack of rights of college athletes and has openly and passionately challenged black college athletes' exploitation by the NCAA and major colleges and universities, such as refusing to compensate student athletes. According to Watkins, coaches are making millions in a sports industry that is deeply rooted in making money on black athletes' backs.

The NCAA has been defining it practices in the courts for some time now on a number of critical issues, the most pressing of which may be the NCAA antitrust law suits. The NCAA has been accused of numerous antitrust violations for using athletes' images and selling them to video game companies without compensating the student-athletes. How could this possibly be true in the United States of America? Rock further posed this critical question in a casual commentary. The main concern according to Chris Rock was, how can amateur sports become so powerful and continue to generate so much money with poor black kids at the center of the equation. It is important to note that black people in general are not making money from college sports, but white people are getting wealthy from black amateur athletes. The truth of the matter is that college and amateur sports exploitation truly runs deep and should at some point be viewed as serious violation of U.S. labor rights laws and should be further examined.

CHAPTER SEVEN

The Historical Significance of HBCU Institutions

"As graduates of this proud university, as young people like those who always stoked the fires of progress, our country is counting on all of you to step forward and help us with the work that remains. We need you."

—First Lady Michele Obama

HBCUs can be traced back to 1837, some twenty-six years before the end of slavery. Richard Humphreys, a Quaker philanthropist, founded the Institute for Colored Youth to train free blacks to become teachers. The school would eventually move from Philadelphia to Cheyney, PA, where it eventually became Cheyney University. By 1902, at least eighty-five schools were set up by white philanthropists, free blacks, states, and churches to educate the sons and daughters of former slaves. It was not until 1954 that the U.S. Supreme Court decision of Brown vs. Board of Education ended "separate but equal" school systems. At that time, HBCUs were option number one for most blacks interested in attending college. Historically, these institutions formed to serve former slaves have evolved to institutions serving the new black middle class to be. Black colleges at the beginning of the new millennium hang on and continue to produce, despite a fierce fight for survival. It is important to note that because of the black college communities, social networks were formed and developed to connect men and women of color from all sectors of the nation. These networks became assets as black political awareness rose and as blacks from HBCUs broke into new categories of jobs, including coaches, teachers, lawyers, business leaders, politicians, and government workers.

Today HBCU campuses continue to make significant contributions to the world. They have produced black astronauts and four-star generals, the former black commander of the Pacific fleet and the chairman of the board of the world's largest brokerage firm and many of others to include bankers, airline pilots, Ph.Ds', computer scientists, college presidents, and several millionaires and billionaires.

One of the most important factors that contributed to the evolution of the HBCUs was the financial support offered by the alumni and black supporters. Millions of dollars donated to HBCUs from noted public figures such as Bill Cosby and Oprah Winfrey have helped to build a new image for many of the black colleges that at one time existed without any real financial backing. Even though some HBCUs remain at the lower end of the scale when it comes to the costs of tuition, they will have to work hard to compete with traditionally white institutions in attracting and educating black students. In an age where more and more black students have choices, many don't want to give up quality. Where many traditionally white institutions have better dormitories with high-speed Internet connections, cable TV, microwaves, and suites with kitchens and private bathrooms, the black colleges will have to keep up and offer similar amenities.

Today's central question continues to resonate: Are HBCUs playing games beyond their limits now that traditionally white institutions seemingly have all of the superstar black student-athletes. HBCUs have not been in the conversation about academic issues until recently. Many people were probably even unaware of HBCUs' history and their valuable contributions to sports. It is unfortunate that year after year a group of black student-athletes enters college to very little excitement. Furthermore, one, two or maybe three athletes will be drafted from that group by the NFL or NBA. For the most part the majority of HBCUs are located in the southeast where large traditionally white institutions' athletic programs dominate. They attract the greatest and most talented black athletes away from HBCUs. Most high-profile black athletes seek to take their talents to Predominantly White Institutions (such as Georgia, Florida, Clemson, South Carolina, North Carolina, Texas, West Virginia,

Oklahoma, Alabama, and Louisiana State), depriving many HBCUs of the talent required to get in the game of big-time sports. Thanks to regular national television appearance, lucrative bowl championships, tournament appearances, and opportunities to play in stadiums that seat 80,000 to 100,000, traditionally white institutions garner millions in payouts at the end of the day. Here is bit of history, it was Dec. 27, 1892 and Livingstone College and Biddle College (now Johnson C. Smith University) met to play the first black college football game. Most of the HBCUs are distributed across four college leagues: the Mid-Eastern Athletic Conference (MEAC), the Southwestern Athletic Conference (SWAC), the CIAA and the Southern Intercollegiate Athletic Conference (SIAC). A handful of other HBCUs play in mainstream conferences—the Ohio Valley Conference (Tennessee State) and the Pennsylvania State Athletic Conference (Cheyney)—or play as independents (Langston).

Exposure is usually an afterthought at HBCUs, despite the contributions of Hall of Famers such as Jerry Rice, Walter Payton, Shannon Sharpe, Richard Dent, and Michael Straham. Most of the top black players now attend major schools in the big-money conferences. HBCUs continue to produce NFL players, in fact a number of HBCU graduates have gone on to play and star in the NFL's biggest game, the Super Bowl. It is unfortunate that HBCU basketball players are less likely to become pro athletes. At one point, during the 1970s and early 1980s, a fair number of NBA players were products of HBCUs. However, they're rarely selected in the draft's high rounds, if they're drafted at all, due to poor athletic exposure. The overall reality is that professional sports organizations are less likely to take a chance on a HBCU student-athlete in favor of students from such schools as Florida, LSU, and Alabama. It is troublesome that the HBCU athletes who make it will be paid, for the most part, the league minimum during first few years. Not much has changed, except that athletic skills of today's athletes may be far greater than those of the past. In the words of Notorious Biggie Smalls, "Things done changed."

Before the black and nonblack athletes became such common accessories at major colleges and universities, the nation's top black student-athletes played at HBCUs. Professional scouts knew where to find them, too, traveling to black schools to watch future all-time greats on the basketball court, the football field, and even the baseball diamond. The

HBCU athletic community is no longer the primary pipeline to the pros for black athletes. Big-time major institutions in the major conferences are regularly featured on television. Big-time high-profile black athlete have largely abandoned HBCUs. Thanks to the passing of the civil rights act, we reclassified the negro athlete as the black athlete. For the black-athlete, this progress included the right to attend any school, not just HBCUs. There are no limits for the prime-time black athlete.

Some concerns within the HBCU athletic community are totally unwarranted. It is horrible that so many HBCUs are failing to adequately educate and graduate black athlete. According to the NCAA's annual Academic Progress Rates (APR), several HBCUs are failing to get the academic job done as it relates to their own black student-athletes. Only a few HBCUs are graduating 70% or more of black student-athletes. HBCUs, more so than traditionally white institutions, must understand that the classroom is the most important battleground, not the field or the court. The APR, meant to measure the eligibility and retention of student-athletes, are calculated for every team of each division. Under the NCAA rules, teams are rewarded for retaining athletes and for ensuring athletes make progress toward degrees and, ultimately, graduation. They are penalized by the NCAA for failing to retain athletes or if their athletes make too little progress toward degrees and ultimately fail to graduate. Penalties include bans on postseason play and a reduction in scholarships.

Based on public information provided by the NCAA during academic years 2006–2007 to 2009–2010, 103 teams at sixty-seven schools were sanctioned for poor academic performance. Of those teams, thirty-three were HBCUs. Of the eight teams that suffered postseason bans, half were from the historically black Southwestern Athletic Conference (SWAC). At first glance, these numbers may not stand out, but they numbers are alarming because, of the 340 schools evaluated for the APR, only 24% fall short. About 7% of HBCUs were reported. HBCUs are disproportionately affected because there are only forty-seven HBCU programs.

Current NCAA President Mark Emmert met with those failing institutions to help them improve retention of student-athletes and help them make progress toward degrees. One of the main obstacles to improving performance among HBCU institutions and their student-athletes is the lack of available and sustainable resources. Predominantly

White Institutions (PWI's) employ an army of academic advisers and professional tutors to help student-athletes. These institutions have substantial infrastructures and support systems in place. President Mark Emmert and former NCAA President Miles Brand should be commended for their efforts, but there is much more work to be done. Many HBCU presidents and athletic directors urge the NCAA to address its formula in cases where a school might be penalized even though many of its student-athletes are academically outperforming nonathletes in the classroom. They also feel that the NCAA should consider that some schools admit borderline students to grant them a second chance, a once in a lifetime opportunity. However, the bottom line is that more resources are needed.

A few years ago, the NCAA has introduced a program called the Supplemental Support Fund, which can provide up to $1 million in grants to "assist low-resource institutions." It is important to note that this is just not for HBCUs, for there are other institutions in academic need as well. According to Walter Harrison, chair of the NCAA Committee on Academic Performance and president of the University of Hartford, the Supplemental Support Fund sounded like a good idea at the time, but the reality is that not every HBCU struggles to achieve an adequate APR. He further stated that those that are falling short need to figure out what the others are doing and follow suit. If and when they receive additional funding from the NCAA, they must develop solid sustainable plans of action or the money will go to waste. It is important to note that one of NCAA president Emmert's ultimate mission is improving academic success for all student-athletes, and he wants every school to focus on that task. At the same time, he realizes that HBCUs are unique in their role, even to this day. Therefore, he is committed to helping them develop solid plans for improvement. The NCAA and President Emmert seem to have a special commitment to work with HBCUs, and the NCAA completely understands that many HBCU institutions have unique different scopes and missions; therefore, the NCAA must use its resources in meaningful ways to help resolved this problem.

Despite limited resources and anemic media exposure, as well as other challenges, these institutions have been the cornerstone of education and development in the black community for more than 150 years. Today, HBCUs continue to face many challenges associated with limited funding.

However, they continue to meet the demands of educating and preparing generations of students and student-athletes of color for great leadership and citizenship; including many national and international leaders from the black community, such as Thurgood Marshall, Oprah Winfrey, and of course, Martin Luther King Jr. On a sad note, far too many HBCUs have, for years, had no sound operational plan for athletics that reflects the realities addressed by most white institutions, small or large. In this day and age, many if not all HBCUs must start thinking seriously about developing sound operational plans for athletics. At the end of day, HBCUs still find themselves largely relegated to the back of the bus in most sports compared to larger and comparable traditionally white institutions. Again, the issue with the APR continues to expose how ill prepared many HBCUs are to deal with the academic, compliance, and eligibility demands of the black student-athlete.

It should be truly embarrassing for HBCUs to be singled out publicly by the NCAA as needing some mercy or special consideration for a lack of proper resources. In many cases, when compared to traditionally white institutions from an overall athletics perspective, some HBCUs are still operating as if they are in the 1960s and 1970s; they are not prepared for prime time competition. Larger HBCUs on average employ just one or two NCAA rules-compliance officers to oversee departments with over 300 athletes, and the academic-support counselors are often on their own, sometimes with little help from coaches. Those coaches have the most influence on their kids, yet they are, themselves, trying to survive. The smaller HBCUs usually employ only one full-time NCAA rules-compliance officer, and academic support/counselors may or may not be available depending on the athletics budget. HBCUs can do a better job to help raise funds: They can effectively and aggressively market and promote their athletic programs to the public and potential sponsors. Too little emphasis has been placed on community and media relations. A sound operational yearly budgeted plan for athletics would greatly enhance, promote, and connect HBCUs with potential sponsors and patrons. This is not a job for one person; it must be a team effort.

In reality, HBCUs have operated largely on pennies and nickels for so long due to segregation from the late 1800s to the early 1960s and even today. Many HBCUs continue to survive and thrive by making the most of limited resources. Merging into the waters of the NCAA in the 1970s and early 1980s was a great thing for HBCUs, but they had no real vision, long-term strategies, or plans to rescue them when the NCAA infraction division came knocking. Therefore, the real question for HBCU athletics should be, at what point will they make the mark and turn the corner to perform academically to the beat of the NCAA drum? HBCU presidents and chancellors need to understand that it is not just about throwing money at athletic directors and head coaches for football and basketball, while diverting funds away from other sports, critical academic support areas, and NCAA rules and compliance. Presidents and chancellors must advance their thinking beyond the old idea that we can get by in other areas by requiring athletic staff to multitask.

There appear to be serious problems in the Southwestern Athletic Conference (SWAC), The SWAC has long-standing history of putting black athlete in the professional ranks. However, in recent years several schools in the SWAC have failed to achieve an adequate APR. HBCU Jackson State University, with its rich football history, continued to fail in this area based on student-athletes' poor academic performance in all sports. The NCAA punished Jackson State with postseason bans, practice-time reductions, including no spring practice for one year, and loss of athletic scholarships. Two other SWAC schools, Grambling (men's basketball) and Southern (football and men's basketball), both find themselves in unpleasant situations resulting from student-athletes' poor academic performance. The MEAC also had several schools punished by the NCAA for student-athletes' poor academic performance.

There are over one hundred conferences recognized by the NCAA but there are only four that are made up of HBCUs. The Central Intercollegiate Athletic Association (CIAA) was founded in 1912 as the Colored Intercollegiate Athletic Association and is the oldest black athletic conference in the nation. The CIAA consists of HBCUs spanning the east coast from Pennsylvania to South Carolina, both private and public colleges and universities with enrollments ranging from 750 to 6,500 students: Bowie State University, Chowan University, Claflin University, Fayetteville State University, Johnson C. Smith University, Elizabeth City State University, Lincoln University of Pennsylvania, Livingstone College, Saint Augustine's College, Shaw University, Virginia State University,

Virginia Union University, and Winston-Salem State University. Chowan University is the only non-HBCU institution.

Over the past ten years, the CIAA has generated over $325 million in economic impact for Charlotte, North Carolina. The CIAA tournament is truly the quintessential cultural expression of any kind, offering specific events beyond basketball that appeal to a diverse demographic of alumni and fans. The CIAA is one of America's oldest athletic conferences. Some of the most rewarding opportunities presented to me personally have come during the CIAA tournament. One example has been the opportunity to talk with some of the former basketball players and hear their oral history about the conference. One of the most interesting stories told to me was a result of the Jim Crow segregation laws that prohibited the conference black players from staying in hotels during road trips in such cities as Greensboro, Winston-Salem, and others. Since they could not stay in hotels, so they would stay on the campus of the home team, eat in the cafeteria and even use the libraries if needed. This also fostered a family foundation among the league's black players. Everyone knew each other on and off the court.

The CIAA has continued to benefit from the stars of the past and present. Several CIAA greats from the past remain a central part of CIAA athletics and administration. Former basketball stars Dr. Al Carter, Dr. Claudie Mackie, and George Williams are all athletic administrators at the institutional level. All three are still working in some capacity to ensure the success of the tournament. All are members of the CIAA Hall of Fame. Dr. Claudie Mackie and George Williams continue to tell stories of their playing days in the conference. They can provide you with brief history lesson on some the greatest players to play in the CIAA conference. Mackie and Williams played against the great Earl "The Pearl" Monroe, Bobby Dandridge and Sam Jones during their college careers. There was no defense by either team. The score was in the hundreds and neither coach would call time out, despite being warned by the official to do so. Moments, later the basketball official called one and told the coaches that they were killing him running up and down the court.

The CIAA is a crown jewel of college sports. The basketball tournament continues to generate national exposure with media and support from major corporations. The tournament and events also attracts former CIAA stars such as Sam Jones, ten-time NBA champion. Alumni greats Earl Monroe, Bob Dandridge, Ricky Mahorn, Charles Oakley, Terry Davis, Ben Wallace, A. J. English, and Ronald Murray all have enjoyed great NBA careers. Another regular attendee to the CIAA tournament is the former Norfolk State University star Pee Wee Kirkland. Pee Wee walked out of the Chicago Bulls training camp to return to his previous life of crime, but then was able to turn his life around again and is now helping kids stay off the streets in upper west side Manhattan. Pew Wee might just be the greatest CIAA players of all time, but his play in the conference was limited. He was a New York City legion and starred in the famed New York City Rocker league.

At the 2017 CIAA Hall of Fame inductions, Pee Wee Kirkland and William Bill Rhoden were both present. I was able to spend some time with both and talk about the CIAA's history. Rhoden was in town to write an article for USA Today about the CIAA tournament and to support his mentee Stephen A. Smith, the co-host of ESPN's First Take, an NBA analyst on SportsCenter, and the host of the Stephen A. Smith Show on Sirius XM's Mad Dog Sports Radio. Smith graduated from Winston-Salem State University. He played basketball under the legendary Clearance "Big House" Gaines. His athletic career was cut short due to injury, but his passion for the CIAA and Winston-Salem State University remain strong.

In addition, to basketball legends, the CIAA tournament has also become a home for popular Hip-Hop artists and comedians. Such contemporary artists like Drake, Yo Gotti, Jeezy, TI, Migos and comedians like Kevin Hart, Mike Epps, and others can been seen around town hosting parties or performing.

The Mid-Eastern Athletic Conference (MEAC) is made up of thirteen HBCUs up and down the Atlantic coast: Bethune-Cookman University, Coppin State University, Delaware State University, Florida A&M University, Hampton University, Howard University, University of Maryland Eastern Shore, Morgan State University, Norfolk State University, North Carolina A&T State University, North Carolina Central University, Savannah State University, and South Carolina State University. In 1969, various intercollegiate athletics personnel met in Durham, NC, to discuss the possibility of forming a new conference for HBCU athletics. The discussions lead to the formation of conference planning committee to fully investigate the idea of a new conference for black student-athletes at HBCUs to showcase their talent. After carefully planning, reviewing, and adopting a program, The Mid-Eastern Athletic Conference (MEAC) was formed with seven institutions: Delaware State College, Howard University, University of Maryland Eastern Shore, Morgan State University, North Carolina A&T State University, North Carolina Central University, and South Carolina State College. The major objective of the conference was to establish, organize, and supervise an intercollegiate athletic program among a compact group of educational institutions with high academic standards and a sound philosophy of cocurricular activities. The conference agreed to seek Division I status for its sports, which it achieved in 1980. The conference was confirmed in 1970, kicking off its first season of competition in football in 1971.

The MEAC sponsors fifteen Division I sports with automatic qualifying bids for NCAA postseason competition in baseball, bowling, men's and women's basketball, men's and women's cross country, football, men's and women's tennis, men's and women's track and field, softball, and volleyball. MEAC student-athletes continue to excel on and off the field and several have been recognized on ESPN's The Magazine/CoSIDA Academic All-America and All-District teams. Several MEAC institutions are excelling in the classroom. The University of Maryland Eastern Shore has been at the top of the conference in graduating student-athletes. From 1999 to 2002 the University of Maryland Eastern Shore reported a 77% graduation success rate, the highest among any MEAC institution for that period. The University of Maryland Eastern Shore has since improved significantly to a 90% graduation success rate; once again ranking as the highest among MEAC institutions spanning the next cohort years. During the 2012 year, Howard University reported an impressive 68% graduation rate for its student-athletes. The cumulative GPA for student-athletes was 3.08; nearly half of all athletes held GPAs above 3.0. The academic improvements by Howard University student-athletes caught the attention of NCAA President Mark Emmitt. He addressed a letter to then Athletic Director Skip Perkins championing accomplishments the academic efforts of the Bison student-athlete. Hampton and Howard University, well known for their high academic standards, continue to graduate less than the University of Maryland Eastern Shore. At the bottom of the MEAC is

Coppin State, which has made some improvement in graduating student-athletes under the leadership of its latest athletic administration.

The Southwestern Athletic Conference (SWAC) was organized exclusively for the purpose of encouraging, promoting, advancing, and conducting intercollegiate sports activities and other recreational and not-for-profit activities among the members of the conference. In 1920, eight men representing six colleges from the state of Texas met to discuss collegiate athletics and the many challenges facing their respective institutions. They founded an athletic league that has slowly become one of the leading sports associations in the world of collegiate athletics, SWAC. The original eight were C. H. Fuller of Bishop College, Red Randolph and C. H. Patterson of Paul Quinn, E. G. Evans, H. J. Evans and H. J. Starns of Prairie View A&M, D. C. Fuller of Texas College, and G. Whitte Jordan of Wiley College. The current SWAC member institutions are now ten HBCUs: Alabama A&M University, Alabama State University, Alcorn State University, University of Arkansas-Pine Bluff, Grambling State University, Jackson State University, Prairie View A&M University, Mississippi Valley State University, Southern University, and Texas Southern University. It is sad to report that the more storied athletic institutions in the SWAC, Grambling State University, Jackson State University, Prairie View A&M University, Southern University, and Texas Southern University have all encountered NCAA problems related to either academic rules or violations related to student-athletes.

The Southern Intercollegiate Athletic Conference (SIAC) was founded in 1913. The conference still flies high as one of the nation's most viable forces in intercollegiate athletics. On December 30, 1913, representatives of nine institutions met at Morehouse College to consider the regulations of intercollegiate athletics among black colleges in the southeast: Alabama State University, Atlanta University, Clark College, Fisk University, Jackson College, Morehouse College, Morris Brown College, Talladega College, and Tuskegee Institute. The representatives formed a permanent organization. The Southeastern Intercollegiate Athletic Conference changed its name The Southern Intercollegiate Athletic Conference in 1929. Two institutions have held continuous membership in the conference: Clark College (now Clark Atlanta University) and Tuskegee University. Other institutions which have held membership are Alabama

A&M University, Allen University, Benedict College, Bethune-Cookman University, Edward Waters College, Fisk University, Florida A&M University, Jackson State University, Knoxville College, Morris Brown College, Rust College, Savannah State University, South Carolina State University, Tennessee State University and Xavier University. The present membership is composed of fourteen different institutions in six states (Alabama, Georgia, Kentucky, South Carolina, Ohio and Tennessee): Albany State University, Benedict College, Claflin University, Clark Atlanta University, Central State University, Fort Valley State University, Kentucky State University, Lane College, LeMoyne-Owen College, Miles College, Morehouse College, Paine College, Spring Hill College, and Tuskegee University.

On a positive note, during the last five years, there has been an increase in graduation rates for HBCUs. However, the overall percentages remain below standards for black students overall. For some time now HBCU's have not done well in terms graduating black student-athletes. More emphasis should be placed on increasing the overall graduation rates among HBCUs. More resources should also be granted to these institutions, which continue to struggle financially year in and year out. Financial factors are undoubtedly a major factor in the low graduation rates at many of the nation's HBCUs. Despite these factors' several HBCUs have made tremendous progress in recent years at increasing the graduation rates of their black students. According to the NCAA, The highest HBCU graduation rate was 79% at Spelman College in Atlanta (GA). The institutions at the bottom of the list are Texas Southern University and the University of the District of Columbia, both graduating an abysmal 11% while Miles College (AL), Rust College (MS), and Coppin State University all come in at 16%. According to statistics published in 2013 in *The Journal of Blacks In Higher Education*, at the top ten Predominantly White Institutions (PWI's) the average graduation rates are 88%.

CHAPTER EIGHT

Black Women and Athletics

"In the field of sports you are more or less accepted for what you do rather than what you are. In sports, you simply aren't considered a real champion until you have defended your title successfully. Winning it once can be a fluke; winning it twice proves you are the best."

—Althea Gibson

It was not until the later part of the 1960s that a handful of women were acknowledged for their contributions to the world of sports. One of the most highly recognized female athletes during this era was a white woman named Joan Weston, a roller derby star and, at one point, the highest paid female athlete in sports. Around 1973, the situation began to change, as Billy Jean King challenged the good old boy status quo when she won the battle of the sexes on national television before thousands. Billie Jean King is an American and the former Worlds' number one professional tennis player. King won thirty-nine Grand Slam titles, including twelve singles, sixteen women's doubles, and eleven mixed doubles titles. In 1973, at age twenty-nine, she won the so-called Battle of the Sexes tennis match against the fifty-five-year-old Bobby Riggs.

It is unfortunate that the efforts such early black women pioneers as Ora Washington and Althea Gibson were not acknowledge enough to change the perceptions of whites and attitudes of sexist males about women's ability to hold their own. I will discuss both Washington and

Gibson later in this section. Even today, most professional women athletes receive little recognition and meager compensation. There is little economic incentive to develop communities able to sustain a women-empowerment athletic organization to support buying and selling teams and sell local and national businesses on sponsorship ads to advance women's sporting organizations. Throughout the history of organized professional women sports in the United States, women have been paid far less than their male counterparts. The most prominent professional women's sports organization to date is the WNBA, which opened in 1997, fifty-one years after the NBA. The WNBA is owned and governed by the NBA Board of Governors. The top women basketball players are paid 60% less than their male counterparts.

Organized team sports are much more difficult to maintain for women. The Women's United Soccer Association became the first American woman's professional soccer league in 2001, but it only lasted for three seasons due to financial challenges. Efforts were made to reopen the pro league in 2004. Worldwide, on average, the top women athletes are unpaid for their athletic participation. Many have to work full-time or part-time jobs while training, practicing, and through actual competition. Professional women sports organizations are still somewhat new to the sports world. As women continue to earn pennies compared to males, women in individual professional sports are likely to earn the most money. According to Forbes Magazine, the top ten professional earnings were in tennis, motorsports, golf, and figure skating. The two Williams sisters, who hail from the urban jungles of Compton California, were the only two black women noted on Forbes Magazine's top-ten list 2010 and 2011 (Table 1).

Table 1: Top-Ten Earning Female Athletes in 2010 and 2011

Rank	Name	Earnings	Sport
2010 FY			
One	Maria Sharapova	$25.0 Million	Tennis
Two	Carolina Wozniacki	$12.5 Million	Tennis
Three	Danica Patrick	$12.0 Million	Motorsport
Four	Venus Williams	$11.5 Million	Tennis
Five	Kim Clijsters	$11.0 Million	Tennis
Six	Serena Williams	$10.5 Million	Tennis
Seven	Kim Yum-Na	$10.0 Million	Figure Skating
Eight	Li Na	$8.0 Million	Tennis
Nine	Ana Ivanović	$6.0 Million	Tennis
Ten	Paula Creamer	$5.5 Million	Golf
2011 FY			
One	Maria Sharapova	$24.5 Million	Tennis
Two	Serena Williams	$20.2 Million	Tennis
Three	Venus Williams	$15.4 Million	Tennis
Four	Danica Patrick	$12.0 Million	Motorsport
Five	Kim Yum-Na	$9.7 Million	Figure skating
Six	Annika Sörenstam	$8.0 Million	Golf (retired)
Seven	Ana Ivanović	$7.2 Million	Tennis
Eight	Jelena Janković	$5.3 Million	Tennis
Nine	Paula Creamer	$5.2 Million	Golf
Ten	Lorena Ochoa	$5.0 Million	Golf (retired)

Forbes ranks only two black women athletes in the top ten for 2010 and 2011, Venus and Serena Williams.

The issue of gender equality among black women in sports continues to be a hot topic. How are black women really doing in a world that places so much emphasis on sexism, racism, and capitalist exploitation? Black women's contributions to the sports world should not be diminished or ignored. Our leading black women athletes were oftentimes noted as the first; therefore, we must be very mindful of their athletic accomplishments.

Take, for example, South Carolina-born Althea Gibson, who is from the small rural community of Silver, South Carolina, less than fifteen miles from my tiny hometown community. Gibson went on to become the first black women to win both the US Open and the Wimbledon Trophy in 1957. As did Jackie Robinson, Gibson became a bigger-than-life public figure at a time in our history when it was unimaginable for any black person, let alone a black women, to reach such heights in sports. It is even more impressive to know that Gibson and her family moved to the north during her childhood years to escape the rigid conditions of the Jim Crow South. Prior to moving to the north, Gibson knew nothing about the game of tennis. Arguably, Althea Gibson is the most celebrated black women athlete in all sports. However, most of her accomplishments have been overshadowed by racism, sexism, and oppression. In her autobiography, *I Always Wanted to be Somebody*, she states that she always desired to be more and do more with her life than just win tennis matches. Like so many blacks, both men and women, Gibson struggled against oppression and racism to achieve any form of success in life. On top of that sexism challenged her humanity, athletic ability, emotional stability, intelligence, and status, not only as an athlete, but as a black women in America.

In 1950, Althea Gibson was the first black women to play tennis at the then-segregated Forest Hill Tennis Tournament. It was truly Gibson who publicly opened the door for other black female athletes, in tennis, track and field, basketball, volleyball, and even lacrosse. Other sports that have seen an increase in black women participation include rowing, golf, and bowling. Following in the footsteps, Althea Gibson, several black women have made names for themselves as college All-Americans, Olympic medalists, national amateurs, and collegiate champions. The early pioneering black women athletes also afforded many blacks women the chance to join the ranks of coaches, athletic administration, officials, and sportscasters. However, it must be noted that only a few black women have been able to migrate into athletic administration, which continues to be dominated by white males and females. White women continue to out rank black women in the areas of athletic administration and coaching.

Bill Rhoden, author of the *Forty Million Dollar Slaves,* told us that the black women encountered the double burden of racism and gender discrimination. For black females, including little black girls, race and gender continue to be a major concern in regards to sport in America. Other notable and successful contemporary black women in sports include Vivian Stringer, Robin Roberts, Cheryl Miller, and two-time Olympic gold medalist and current University of South Carolina head women's basketball coach, Dawn Staley. These women continue to demonstrate the excellence of black women in sports. In 2017, Dawn Staley, was just selected to coach the 2020 U.S. Women's Olympic basketball team in Tokyo. Less than a month later, Staley became only the second black female to win the NCAA Women's basketball title in the history of women's basketball. Staley successfully lead the University of South Carolina lady Gamecocks to the school's first-ever women's national title in 2017. It is unfortunate that blacks in general, and particularly black women, are negatively impacted by sexism, racism, and exploitation. At the end of the day, sexism, racism, and exploitation of black women in sports remains the common denominator. To be honest about the matter, this problem is all heavily motivated by capitalism in the form of exploitation of the black women athlete.

Take, for instance, Althea Gibson who played at one of most prestigious tennis tournaments in the world. She was earning peanuts compared to the tennis stars of today. Gibson came from a very poor family; her father was garage attendant, and Althea dropped out of school to work to help the family. So you see it is truly amazing that she actually found her way to the game of tennis. It was unfortunate that Gibson, who accomplished so much, never actually received her fair share in terms of compensation for her talents and labor. As an athlete in her prime, she really never received any major lucrative endorsement opportunities. Althea Gibson's historic efforts helped define and establish a place for black women athletes to make a name for themselves and earn beyond a fair wage for their talents and labor. Over the years, black women have progressed in sports. Gibson, who won at Wimbledon, received no monetary prize for her efforts. In contrast, either of the Williams sisters might earn up to half a million for winning or losing, not to mention their commercial endorsements.

Opportunities for black women today are seemingly more abundant. The visibility and opportunities afforded to black women today continue to increase; however, there is still much work to be done to increase the pool of black women athletes not just in athletic competitions, but in the all areas of sports: from the courts, to broadcast booths, to the upper levels of athletic administration. Black women athletes continue to face sexism, racism, and exploitation ideologies. It is important to note that black women in sports always remain somewhat marginalized because of the color of their skin.

During Gibson's era and today, it is not at all popular to celebrate the black women, but it does appear popular to belittle the efforts of black women in sports. Even today the majority of black women in sports are marginalized by the overall lack of positive celebrations. The black women athlete is less likely to be photographed in a positive light. The black women athlete is less likely to be appear in popular sporting magazines such as *Sports Illustrated* wearing swim wear. Black women cheerleaders are less likely to be photographed for popular magazines, both professional and collegiate. This is nothing more than commercial racism and sexism, which is being used to further define and marginalize the black women athlete.

Despite all of the challenges and frustrations black women athletes faced both in the past and the present day, they were somehow able to make remarkable strides in a sports world that continues to be dominated by men. The few well-known women of color who have come to play and stay have opened the door for more women of color. Furthermore, more and more women of color are now pursuing a college education, traveling the world, and receiving global acclaim for their involvement to sports, which is a wonderful thing. In their contributions to *Disentangling Consciencism*, McClendon III and Ferguson II stated that overt forms of racism, sexism, and classism have negatively impacted black women in sports. They also discussed how historically the struggles of the black women in sports have been directly linked the slave plantation experiences as it relates to race, sexism, and capitalist exploitation. To be honest, black women in general have always found themselves in a struggle with America's overt sexist, racist, and capitalist exploitation. Long before the black women was first introduced to the world of sports, they were preoccupied by extreme experiences of poverty within the context racism, sexism, and capitalist exploitation. Black women and sports was a complete afterthought, until someone discovered that money could be made by allowing black women to join sports.

Black women like Gibson were compelled to begin working early in their lives due to the extreme levels of poverty in which they lived. Many of these girls came from poor rural farming communities where they had to help to put food on the table. You can imagine there was no time for sports of any kind. It was not uncommon for these girls to work fourteen hours per day. In the south, there was no time for any leisure activities. Working to help the family in whatever capacity was the sporting event of day. Prior to 1917, baseball, horse racing, and boxing were the main sports for blacks. There were definitely no women in these sports. The entry point into the world of sports for many black women athletes can be traced back to the rural southern plantations experiences or the North's poverty-ridden urban cities. Large urban communities such as New York, Chicago, and Washington, DC, provided a number of athletic opportunities for young black girls, who may have never considered attending college.

Althea Gibson was born in the poor rural south and lived on a dirt road prior to moving to New York City. She did not learn the game of tennis in the south. That came only when she arrived in New York City. Another great black female athlete who unlocked the door for other aspiring young black girls was Wilma Glodean Rudolph an Olympic champion. She was the fastest woman in the world and competed in two Olympic games, 1956 and 1960. In the 1960 Summer Olympics in Rome, Rudolph became the first American woman to win three gold medals in track and field during a single Olympic games. As a track and field champion, she elevated women's track to a major presence in the United States.

Yet another early pioneering black women, Alice Coachman, was the fifth of ten children. Coachman was born on November 9, 1923, in Albany, Georgia, a predominantly black small town in southwest Georgia. As a child, Alice was considered a tomboy, but her father, influenced by society's reluctance to accept female athletes and fearing for her safety as a black in a segregated society, initially discouraged her from participating in any sports. However, she was encouraged by her fifth-grade teacher and her aunt. Due to the lack of integrated sporting and training facilities, coachman was forced to practice on the dirt roads and hills surrounding rural Albany, Georgia. What was so remarkable about Coachman was that she mainly trained without shoes, which added to her toughness and endurance. After high school, Coachman went on to attend Tuskegee Institute, where she became a track star. She went on to become the first black female athlete of any nation to win an Olympic gold medal and also was the first American female to win an Olympic medal in track and field. In 1952, Alice Coachman became the first black woman to sponsor a national product by signing an endorsement deal with Coca Cola. Coachman set an Olympic record with a high jump leap of 5' 6-1/8". Upon returning to the United States, Coachman and several other black Olympians met with President Harry Truman at the White House, but when Coachman returned to her hometown she was subjected to the racially discriminatory laws of the south.

The two HBCUs leading the way in recruiting black females to complete and booster their athletic teams are Tennessee State University and Tuskegee University. Located in the south, they had easy access to a rural population of natural female athletes. For the most part these young ladies came from poor rural southern communities, where they often lived and, in some cases, worked on the farm with family members prior to and during college. It was not uncommon for these young ladies to return home during summer break to help out where needed. The poor and oppressive social conditions in which many of these ladies lived often produced women who had no proper attire or even the appropriate athletic shoes needed to compete. Alice Coachman ran without shoes in a number of sporting events.

To understand the cultural ideological aspect of the black women athlete, we must first consider the major limitations placed upon them within the context of the sporting world in general. The black women's physical appearance was so denigrated by non-blacks that one often failed to consider just how popular and attractive they really were, while still maintaining truly feminine soft ladylike ways. Certainly, a more relevant question today is whether or not the black women athlete is as marketable as black male athletes. Another critical question that continues to be discussed is their femininity and sexuality. Similar to the female rappers, to appear authentic, they must be less feminine and more masculine to be completely respected as women athletes. Sometimes, it appears that black women athletes are automatically lumped into a nonfeminine role, some may say "mannish," to be somewhat accepted into the sports world.

Oh, how things have changed, at one point in sports, female athletes could not be too cute, too pretty, or too feminine if they wanted to be truly accepted as black women athletes. Take, for instance, WNBA player Skylar Diggins, who was featured on the Sports Illustrated Summer 2014 swimsuit edition. Diggins played for the WNBA Tulsa Shock at the time and graduated from Notre Dame as the school's all-time scoring leader. Diggins is represented by Shawn Carter, aka Jay-Z, the rap mogul and entrepreneur. Skylar Diggins has gotten her fair share of rap admirers from Lil' Wayne to Chris Brown; even Drake has jumped on the bandwagon of late. On the flip side there is Brittney Griner, a 6'-8" center in the WNBA. She played here college basketball at Baylor University in Waco, Texas. Griner was the first NCAA basketball player in the history of the sport to score 2,000 points and block 500 shots. It does appear that times have changed; Griner wears a men's US size 17 shoe and has an amazing 86" arm span. She was the first openly gay athlete to sign with Nike. Once Griner graduated from Baylor University, she decided that it was time to be completely open and honest about her sexuality, regardless of the consequence and revealed her lesbian status to the world prior to her WNBA draft date.

Many of the cultural ideologies found in women's athletics are deeply rooted in the old traditions of race, sex, gender, and cultural values associated with slavery. Furthermore, many of these cultural ideologies are connected to the cultural expressions of one's personal experience: Language, attitude, behavior, and cultural values are all connected to slavery. One can also observe the positive cultural values that both black women and men athletes possess. These cultural values include courage, independence, resilience, and toughness. Contributing to the increase in black women in athletics is their ability to understand how to employ their physical and mental prowess in sports.

However, the fundamental values conflict continues to affect black women and men, which can produce levels of cultural conflict tension or problems. One of the primary conflicts is that of white acceptance in the world organized sports. This brings us back to issue of cultural racism, gender discrimination, and sexism that ultimately govern the business of sports. During slavery, black women were good enough to cook, clean, and care for the slave master's children and even bare their children. They can now play various sports in front of thousands of majority white fans. As I stated earlier, some things never change. Black women athletes' achievements must be attributed to acceptance and approval by both the white and black worlds. This was the key to advancing the efforts of black women in sports.

Individuals from both races were, to varying degrees, opposed to allowing women to play sports. This resulted in the development of Title IX Legislation with its emphasis on gender equality intended to increase and promote women's involvement and participation. Some of the issues raised by men concerned female athletes' femininity, especially black women. As more and more black women began to engage in sports, more and more of their feminine values, attitudes, and behaviors have come into question. Is she a man or a woman? The term many use is "mannish."

Another conflict is the poor understanding of the majority of the black community who opposed the participation of black girls in sporting events. They felt that by having black women pursuing athletic careers would ultimately damage their ability to reproductive, promote sexual decadence, and thus challenge their natural gender differences. Making the adjustment to the culture of sports, coupled with being a female with feminine mannerism was not at all an easy transition for black women. This proves to be a real test in terms of the mannish stereotypes as a result of participating in sports. Not to mention the color of their skin, which further reinforces the issues of race, gender inequality, class, and sexism. For the most part, black women athletes struggled and suffered during the early days, and even today, from what I describe as the 3-D Theory (devalued, disrespected, and discriminated). This theory implies that the black woman athlete encountered this level of treatment from both blacks and whites. Those who objected to their participation in sports dominated by men seek to deny black women the opportunity to play sports. To be treated fairly, respected, and valued is still today somewhat a serious dilemma confronting the black woman heterosexual athlete.

The black female athlete appears to be trapped in a large web that is controlled and governed by racial gender constructs, sexual orientation, and exploitation coupled with oppressive ideologies. We must now pay close attention to how things have changed in women's sporting terminology. Through various social constructs for years, we have consistently made references to outstanding black women athletes being mannish. We now refer to their talents as athleticism, which also reinforces the 3-D Theory of devaluing their femininity. It appears that being an athletic woman is less than being a woman. When a female athlete decides to show off her feminine, she struggles for acceptance once again. Now, truth be told, there are some women athletes who have no desire at all to be have their feminine qualities valued and respected. On the flip side, there are some women athletes who have successfully balanced their athletic talents and their feminine qualities. As a notable example, consider the Williams sisters. They both have an athletic body similar to that of a male warrior, yet they are as attractive and feminine outside of competition as any other woman.

Some HBCUs have seen fit to offer black girls the opportunity to not only participate in organized sports, but to earn a college education alone the way. From a historical standpoint, there was not an abundance of blacks in general who went to college, and there were even fewer black women college graduates. This sport-participation opportunity allows a number of women of color the chance to advance athleticism and career development in any number of chosen academic paths. In a variety of sporting arenas, including track and field, volleyball, basketball, tennis, softball, golf, and swimming, have attracted the attention of women of color. Other sports that blacks are now participating in include lacrosse, soccer, bowling, and equestrian sports. The history of Gibson and Rudolph has been told, but each time it is told something new is learned about the great efforts of black women athletes. The game of basketball has produced a number of outstanding women athletes. The more contemporary black women of sports are often cited on ESPN and sports centers, but little attention is directed to legends of the past. Why are there not more stories and documentaries like ESPN 30–30 telling the story black women pioneers in the world of sports? One such story that deserves to be told involves Evelyn "Sweetie" Johnson, the younger sister of Ervin "Magic" Johnson who starred at the University of South Carolina from 1979 to 1983. Like her brother Magic, Sweetie ran the team as a guard.

Before there was Althea Gibson or Wilma Rudolph, those in the sports world knew of Ora Washington, by some standards the best women athlete ever. Ora Washington was born in southern Virginia in 1899. Her family moved to Philadelphia in search of better opportunities during her early teen years. Washington was an Olympic track star in the 1930s, one of the nation's top basketball players, a swimmer, and champion golfer in the 1940s. She stared above other athletes in both tennis and basketball where, just as with baseball prior to Jackie Robinson, there was no place for the black athlete. This resulted in the formation of various small sporting leagues for black-athletes. One such organization was the American Tennis Association.

Washington played her first organized sporting event at the age of twenty-one. Her first love was tennis and, within one year, Washington was so good she entered a national tournament for black players. In here first five seasons as a pro, she won multiple titles and held the American Tennis Association's National crown from 1929 to 1936. Losing was apparently not an option for Washington, because she was undefeated for years. By the time of her retirement in 1940, Washington had won an amazing eight singles, twelve doubles, and three mixed doubles championships. As great as Washington was, she was never allowed the opportunity to play the world's best white player of that era, Helen Wills Moody. From the mid-1920s through the early 1930s, Moody ruled the world of the prestigious Wimbledon and Forest Hills., but she refused to play against Washington. However, Washington's efforts did not go unnoticed. Her success on the tennis courts encouraged President Roosevelt and his administration to construct hundreds of public tennis courts in urban communities where the game was unfamiliar. Such future tennis greats as Arthur Ashe, Althea Gibson, and the Williams sisters would develop their tennis skills on these courts.

Washington's efforts not only opened the door for blacks to play the US Open and Wimbledon, it also made history as several persons of color would go on to win at these most prestigious tennis events. After Washington had achieved all that she could on the tennis courts, she turned her attention and interest to basketball, playing center for the Germantown Hornets and the Philadelphia Tribune. Many considered Washington to be as good as men in the game. Washington also went on to become an outstanding swimmer and baseball player. Throughout Washington's athlete career, she held a job as a domestic worker in order to survive. In 1940, she finally retired from all athletic competition and went into business before purchasing an apartment complex. In 1971, Washington died in near obscurity. It is unfortunate that she was almost unknown outside of the black community.

Another outstanding black female athlete who is almost forgotten today was Inez Patterson. She was recognized by many sports experts as arguably the most versatile women in the history of the state of Pennsylvania. Patterson enrolled in Temple University in 1929 and graduated from Temple University in 1934. While at Temple, Patterson lettered and made the all-collegiate teams in field hockey four consecutive years. She also lettered and made all-collegiate in tennis, basketball, track, volleyball, and dancing. After graduation from Temple University, Patterson participated in a number of local and national championship events. After college Patterson devoted much of her professional career to developing and training young girls of color in recreation and physical education at YMCAs in Southwest Belmont, Orange, Newark, Montclair, Jersey City, and New York City. Patterson was appointed as director of the American Tennis Association in 1938. Patterson was truly a phenomenal black woman athlete.

Despite the many accomplishments of black women who have participated in sports, from general recreational activities to intercollegiate athletics and the professional ranks, black women, and women in general continue, to lag far behind both black and white males. It is unfortunate that black women have been completely relegated to second-class status. With the focus once again on class, race, and gender, the struggle continues for most women of color. There are still too few opportunities for the black women athletes to fairly participate beyond amateur or college. Of course, the WNBA oversees a professional league willing to accept black women, but there are only a few slots. There are just too few professional sporting opportunities for women in general. Beyond basketball, women's professional sports include soccer, golf, softball, horse racing, tennis, volleyball, and motorsports.

There are several critical questions to consider, the first being what would the black women athlete do after her amateur career ended? The second question to think about would be how women's sports has grown to become more popular to the world? Unfortunately, the opportunities for high-profile sports broadcaster and coaching jobs are afforded to few women of color. Only a small handful of blacks have risen to ranks of on-air media analysis, coaching, or athletic administration at any level: high school, college, and the professional ranks. This leads to another important concern for women. Why are there so few black women sportscasters? Black women working in sports and in the media: Who are they and how did they get there? To be continued in the next chapter.

CHAPTER NINE

Black Women Sportscasters

"There has been a lot of progress, but there is still much that needs to be done, and so while you need to celebrate the progress, and the things that are moving forward, you can't lose sight of all the work that needs to be done. I look around and I see that there is less debris, but I see that there is still debris that needs to be cleared."

—Robin Roberts

The important role that black women sportscasters have played over the years cannot be overstated. They have forever influenced and changed the way sports are presented. Another trailblazing black female who was truly ahead of her time was none other than Jayne Kennedy. In 1970, she became the first black Miss Ohio. Jayne advanced as one of the top fifteen finalists in the 1970 Miss America competition. Many may not know that Kennedy became one of the first black woman sportscasters in the country. Eight years after the Miss America pageant, Kennedy was a starring host on CBS Networks' NFL Today. Kennedy was also the first woman to join the staff of CBS Sports. In 1978, Kennedy became one of the first women to enter the sportscasting business. She joined the cast of NFL Today as a studio analyst during the years when the Pittsburgh Steelers (Super Bowl XIII & XIV), the Oakland Raiders (Super Bowl XV), and the San Francisco 49ers (Super Bowl XVI) ruled the NFL. Kennedy was also only one of only a handful of black actresses to consistently get work in the 1970s. The beautiful Jayne regularly graced the front pages of *Ebony Magazine* and *Jet Magazine* during the 1980s. In 1981, she made history yet again when she became the first black actress to make the front cover of Playboy Magazine. Copies of the magazine immediately sold out as soon as the issue hit the stands. Despite Playboy's image, there were absolutely no nude photos of Jayne in that edition. As we sit by our TVs, captivated by the world of sports, including hoops, football, baseball, tennis, and even soccer, not to mention the drama and scandals associated with sports, we must be truly inspired by the efforts of our leading ladies who make tuning in relevant for blacks who love sports. Altogether thirteen black women who are just as addicted to sports as the average male have been able to put their unique spin on sports. Here is a look at the thirteen black women who have changed the game as we know it.

Pam Oliver is a former college track and field All-American in the 400 meters and mile relay at Florida A&M University. While at Florida A&M University, Oliver earned her bachelor's degree in broadcast journalism which prepared her for what she does today. Oliver is a veteran reporter on FOX Sports is a fixture on the sidelines of NFL and NBA games and arguably the first black women sportscaster to work the NFL sidelines. Pam began her broadcast career in 1985 after graduating from college. Her first job was in Albany, Georgia, as a news reporter. Within one year, Oliver was on the move, having landed a job in Huntsville, Alabama. In 1988, Oliver relocated to Buffalo, New York, and two years later she moved to Tampa, Florida, when she got her big break in sports as a local sports anchor. In 1993, Oliver joined the ESPN television network, but the executives from Fox Sports called her in 1995, and she became not just a sideline reporter for football, but the first black women sideline reporter for any major professional televised sport. Oliver teamed up with the network's top broadcast duo Joe Buck and Troy Aikman. In 2005, Oliver again on the move joined the TNT network as sideline reporter for NBA playoff coverage. Despite Oliver's age, she is truly a pioneer in the world of black women broadcasters. It is worth noting that Oliver has been replaced by Erin Andrews, a white female, but she has been reinstated by the network as an on-air sportscaster.

Lisa Salters is a confident and competent black women and a former collegiate women's basketball player. She was one of the first to interview Los Angeles Clippers owner Donald Sterling's wife after the story broke about his racial remarks about blacks. Before covering the NBA and NFL for over a decade, Salters graduated from Penn State University in 1988 with a bachelor's degree in broadcast journalism. While at Penn State, she played guard for the Lady Lions basketball team. Salters holds the distinction of being the shortest player in school history at only 5' 2". Salters joined ESPN and ESPN on ABC in the year 2000. One of the early highlights of Salters' career was when she was selected to cover the 2006 Winter Olympics in Turin Italy. Other high points of Salter's career include covering the trials of former Carolina Panther Rae Carruth, the Oklahoma City Bomber, O.J. Simpson, and Matthew Shepard's murders. In the profession of sports, Salters is not just your average sportscaster who loves sports. She is a serious journalist with a true passion for sports. In addition to covering the 2006 Winter Olympics, Salters has also covered the FIFA World Cup.

Before joining ESPN, Salters, was correspondent for ABC World News with Peter Jennings and worked for ESPN's *Outside the Lines.* In the spring of 2006, Salters was selected to cover the NBA finals as a sideline reporter for ABC sports. In 2009, Salters added radio to the list of her accomplishments, when she covered the NBA on radio. It is not uncommon to see Salters covering college basketball, football, and even Monday Night NFL football. She has also served as a correspondent for ESPN award- winning newsmagazine, *E: 60,* and she was nominated for a Sports Emmy for the ESPN story Ray of Hope.

Next on the list is none other than Cheryl Miller, who may be one of the greatest, if not the greatest female basketball player in modern history. Miller is the older sister of former NBA great Reggie Miller. She was a big star at USC (Southern Cal) into the early 1980s with the two McGee sisters long before opportunities such as the WNBA materialized. Miller returned to USC to coach from 1993 to 1995. In 1997, she joined the Phoenix Mercury of the WNBA as the general manager and head coach until the 2000 season when she became a staple on NBA sidelines. As a two-time basketball Hall of Famer, she has been involved in the game for over two decades. Miller served as a sideline reporter for the NBA on TNT's Thursday night doubleheaders and during the 2008–2009 NBA season as a reporter and on-air analyst. Miller made history as the first black women to provide critical analysis about men's basketball on television. In 1995, Miller joined Turner Sports, which was ahead of pack in sports broadcasting with the exception of the big three networks (NBC, ABC and CBS). While at Turner, Miller was an on-air analyst and reporter for the NBA and TBS which just happened to be owned by Ted Turner. In 1996, Miller became the first black female to ever do the play-by-play of a national televised NBA game. Prior to joining the ranks of professional sports broadcasting, Miller worked as a reporter for ABC/ESPN from 1987 to 1993. She was also a reporter for ABC's Wide World of Sports and a basketball commentator for the network's college basketball telecast. Miller returned to coaching when she was named the head coach of tiny NAIA Langston University in 2014.

Jemele Hill has really made a name for herself in the world of sports. This Detroit native lives and breathes sports, co-hosting both ESPN2's *Numbers Never Lie* and the *His & Hers* sports podcast. Jemele Hill cohosts *SC6 with Michael & Jemele* on ESPN. Previously, Hill and Smith co-hosted ESPN2's *His & Hers,* a daily sports discussion program. She joined ESPN.com in 2006 as a national columnist before making appearances on television, including *SportsCenter, First Take, Around the Horn, The Sports Reporters* and *Outside the Lines. SC6* is one of the most watched sports programs on the ESPN network. The on-camera chemistry between Jemele and Michael is amazing. To say that Jemele and Michael have taken sports reporting to a new level is an understatement. The duo began reporting sports news by incorporating some of the latest Hip-Hop and popular-culture spoofs, such as Anchorman, Boyz n the Hood and Empire. Sports, social commentary, and pop culture meet on their show. The show explores the relationships between athletes and coaches, fans and teams, men and women.

Hill graduated from Michigan State University with a degree in journalism and a minor in Spanish. After college, Hill came south and worked as sports writer for the Raleigh-based *News and Observer* newspaper. Hill has also worked as a sports writer with the *Detroit Free Press.* Prior to joining ESPN in 2006, Hill worked with the *Orlando Sentinel.* Shortly after joining the ESPN family, Hill could be seen regularly on *SportsCenter, ESPN First Take, Outside the Lines,* and *The Sports Reporter.* She has quickly made a name for herself in sports.

For her outstanding service in the arena of sports, Hill received the

McKenzie Cup award, and in 2007, she received the Best American Sports Writing award. However, during the 2008 NBA playoffs, Hill was suspended for referring to Adolf Hitler in the context of the Boston Celtics. In 2009, Hill received yet another reprimand for her comparison of John Calipari to Charles Manson. Hill's flamboyant style of writing and reporting sports has been criticized by many, but her authentic urban style has changed the way sports is now being seen and reported.

Cari Champion made a name for herself in the sports world sitting between Stephen A. Smith and Skip Bayless daily on ESPN's *First Take*. Champion has the unenviable task of tempering passionate discussions between Smith and Bayless. Champion is a 1998 graduate of the University of California at Los Angeles. She holds a degree in English with a minor in mass communication. Champion's journalism career began while in college at UCLA, she was writer for the *Daily Bruin*. Prior to ESPN, Champions career took her from California to Washington DC for an internship with CNN, and finally to West Virginia where she landed her first reporting job. Champion has also worked as a reporter in West Palm Beach, Florida, and served as an anchor and reported for the Tennis Channel.

According to Champion, while working at the Tennis Channel, she discovered a real love for the game of tennis. While covering women's tennis, she also spent time with the Williams sisters, which added to her love and respect for the game. It was not until 2012 that Champion joined ESPN on *First Take*. Champion beat out Jemele Hill for the spot and the rest is history. Champion was born and raised in Southern California, where she grew up loving sports, especially her hometown LA. Lakers.

Next is the smooth and gifted Sage Steele, a 1995 graduate of Indiana University. Sage is the product of biracial parents. Her father was the first black man to play varsity football at West Point during the 1960s. Steele's very first sports reporting job was for one of the CBS affiliates in South Bend, Indiana. After leaving South Bend, Sage moved to Indianapolis, where she was the weekend, weekday, and morning sports reporter. For a brief time, Steele worked in Tampa, with an ABC affiliate. In Florida, she met and teamed up with Jay Crawford who went on to host ESPN *SportsCenter*. Before leaving Florida, Steele joined Fox Sports Florida as a reporter covering professional sports in central Florida.

After leaving sunny and warm Florida, Steele headed north for the Mid-Atlantic. She was the central newscaster for the NFL Baltimore Ravens. It was not until the spring of 2007, that Steele officially joined ESPN *SportsCenter*. During Steele's tenure at ESPN, she has been quite busy. She has served as co-host of *SportsCenter, and* contributed to *First Take, Mike & Mike in the Morning,* and *SportsNation*. During the 2012 and 2013 NBA finals, Steele hosted *SportsCenter's* daytime reporting. Steele has also hosted *NBA Countdown,* another popular ESPN and ABC broadcast.

Josina Anderson showed her talents in front of the camera live as a correspondent in Cleveland when she reported that LeBron James was returning to his home town in hopes of bring the city a world championship. Anderson was the first to break the story to the world. She is a former college athlete herself, who loves the world of sports. Since joining ESPN, she has been a correspondent for the network covering the NFL and NBA. The addition of Anderson, further strengthened ESPN's commitment to diversity among women of color.

Prior to coming on board with ESPN, Anderson worked in the Chicago market, mainly, as a reporter covering the NBA and NFL. Anderson has reported several impressive sports stories. During her career she has undertaken the investigative-reporter path. Anderson has also been at the forefront of reporting on important issues outside the lines of sports, such as drug testing and sports, contract signings, and the unfortunate death of several former professional sports figures. Anderson's contributions to Showtime's *Inside the NBA* are yet another of her accomplishments. Keep your eyes on Josina Anderson. The future is sure to present great things for such as young and brilliant sportscaster.

Kristina Pink covers the Los Angeles Clippers as a sideline reporter for Fox Sports. Pink joined the Fox family in 2012, serving as both a sideline reporter for Los Angeles Clippers telecasts on *Prime Ticket* and as an NFL sideline reporter on Fox alongside play-by-play announcer Ron Pitts and analyst Mike Martz. Prior to joining Fox Sports, Kristina worked in the New Orleans market and as sports anchor at WDBD Fox 40 News in Jackson, Mississippi. While in Jackson, she covered a number of major sporting events, but nothing more exciting than the Saints' Super Bowl XLIV victory over the Colts in her hometown of Miami, Florida. She began her broadcasting career in college doing feature stories on University of Florida athletics. Kristina also served as a sportscaster for the university's television station, WUFT, and campus radio station, WRUF-AM 850. In October 2009, Pink graduated from the University of Florida with a Bachelor's degree in telecommunications.

Christy Winters-Scott, one of the most outstanding college basketball analysts in the game, is a native of Virginia, where she starred on the basketball courts. After high school, Winters-Scott accepted a basketball scholarship to play at the University of Maryland College Park. Before leaving College Park, she ranked among the university best. Winters-Scott was instrumental in the University of Maryland women's basketball team reaching the final four and the university eighth ACC Championship in school history.

Christy Winters-Scott covers basketball for ESPN, Fox Sports South, Raycom, and CBS Radio. Winters-Scott is a regular color analyst for the ACC and SEC network. Because of her remarkable knowledge of women's basketball, she has moved on to cover the NCAA women's basketball tournament. In addition, Winters-Scotts is also the on-court color analyst for the WNBA's Washington Mystics. She is also the host of the Mystics' pre-and postgame shows.

As a senior, she was named First Team All ACC and Kodak All-East Region. After graduating from Maryland, Winters-Scott wanted to continue competing, but the WNBA was not yet in existence, so Winters-Scott headed overseas where she spent a year playing in Pistoia, Italy and another two years in Fribourg, Switzerland. During her final professional season in Switzerland, she averaged thirty-seven points and twelve rebounds per game, and had a career high of forty-eight points while competing for the Euro Cup. Winters-Scott then changed her focus to coaching and broadcasting and became an assistant coach for George Mason from 1993 to 1997, Maryland from 1997 to 2002, and Georgetown from 2004 to 2005. In 2005, Winters-Scott departed Georgetown to accept a head coaching position for her alma mater (South Lakes High School). One night a week, Winters-Scott produces and broadcasts shows for the Roundball Report, on CTV76 in Maryland. The Roundball Report shows quickly caught the attention of the DC broadcasting market. As a result of her loyalty to the profession, she has drawn the praise and attention of Michael Wilbon a veteran black male sportscaster. Since joining the Mystics, Winters-Scott is now covering the NBA's Washington Wizards.

Winters-Scott broadcasts twenty to thirty college games a year and all Mystics and Wizards TV games. On top of that, she coaches her alma mater. Winters-Scott also holds an impressive resume of awards: ACC fiftieth Anniversary Team, South Lakes Athletic Hall of Fame, University of Maryland Hall of Fame, ACC Women's Basketball Legend, and Shirley Povich Center for Sports Journalism Distinguished Terrapin Award. She was most recently recognized by *Essence Magazine* as one of the top twelve black female sports reporters in the country.

Keli Fulton, a seasoned sports reporter, currently works as an anchor and reporter for Comcast's *SportsNet Central* covering the NFL and NBA. Fulton is a television veteran with more than twelve years of experience. She was a welcome addition to the team of expert anchors, reporters, analysts, and writers that provide comprehensive regional sports coverage for Comcast *SportsNet*. Fulton joined Comcast *SportsNet* after three years with WPTV-TV (NBC) and WFLX-TV (FOX) in West Palm Beach, Florida, where she served as a news and traffic anchor. Prior to that, she was a sports anchor and reporter for WDSU-TV (NBC) in New Orleans from 2007 to 2011. There, she covered the Hornets' trip to the NBA's Western Conference Finals, Louisiana State University's football and baseball national championship teams, and the Saints' victory in Super Bowl XLIV. She began her television career as a reporter covering high school sports for Cal-Hi Sports in Northern California. Fulton is a native of Fort Worth, Texas, and a graduate of Whittier College, where she studied theatre arts and communications. The final word on the street is that she can also sing the hell out of the National Anthem.

Maria Taylor might just be the baby of the bunch, but this former University of Georgia athlete has made the move from the volleyball and basketball courts to ESPN as sideline reporter. Taylor, is not hard to miss at an amazing 6' 2". Truly, she can see a lot, she is usually one of the tallest people on the sidelines. Taylor's height is truly an asset for her sports career.

As a former volleyball star at the University of Georgia, Taylor has worked tremendously to advance the fan base for women's volleyball. She has been the number-one ambassador for the sport and Taylor has successfully used her ambassador status to endorse volleyball. Taylor, quickly became a household name on ESPN's Wednesday night volleyball, with her ability to analyze the game and deconstruct the play of some of the nations' best colligate volleyball players. Taylor's overall commitment to promoting volleyball to a new generation of fan is what makes her a champion sportscaster. By all accounts, Taylor, credits being a former NCAA student-athlete as the foundation for her current success as a sportscaster for ESPN and the SEC network. Before, the SEC network went on the air, they decided to reached out to one of their very own, none other than Maria Taylor.

Kara Marie Lawson is yet another exemplary black woman in sports. Lawson attended the University of Tennessee and played for the legendary Pat Summit. She was an outstanding collegiate player, which paved her way to the WNBA. Lawson was also a member of the 2008 women's basketball team, winning an Olympic gold medal in Beijing. Shortly after joining the WNBA, Lawson, earned the opportunity to serve as a color analyst. She has not looked back since. Lawson has served as an analyst for ESPN covering both the NBA and college basketball. Many may not know that in 2007, Kara Marie Lawson became the first women to work as a national broadcast analyst for the NBA. Lawson's love for sports and her passion have not gone unnoticed. She is becoming a household name as an outstanding broadcast analyst for both men and women athletes.

Finally there is none other than the one and only Robin Roberts. She is a former basketball standout at Southeastern Louisiana University. Roberts became a household name on ESPN; now millions wake up to her on ABC Good Morning America as one of the lead newscasters. Robin Renee Roberts, born in Alabama, grew up in Pass Christian, Mississippi, where she played basketball and tennis among other sports. Roberts attended Southeastern Louisiana University in Hammond, Louisiana, graduating cum laude in 1983 with a degree in communication. Roberts followed in the footsteps of her older sister, Sally-Ann Roberts, who was an anchor at the local CBS affiliate in New Orleans. Roberts began her career in 1983 as a sports anchor and reporter in her home state of Mississippi at WDAM-TV in Hattiesburg, Mississippi. In 1984, she moved to the coastal community of Biloxi, Mississippi. In 1986, she moved into the world of sportscasting and reporting for WSMV-TV in Nashville, Tennessee. From

1988 to 1990, Roberts worked as a sports anchor and reporter at the local Atlanta, Georgia, station, WAGA-TV, while also hosting on local radio station V-103 FM in Atlanta. In February 1990, Roberts joined ESPN as a national sportscaster and stayed until 2005.

At ESPN Roberts made a real name for herself, where she became well known on the nightly SportsCenter telecast for her catchphrase, "Go on with your bad self!" In 2005, Roberts moved on to work for one of the big three, ABC News, specifically as a featured reporter for the early morning *Good Morning America* show. For several years, Roberts worked at both ESPN and *Good Morning America,* serving primarily as the news anchor at *Good Morning America.* Shortly after her arrival at ABC, Roberts was promoted to coanchor of *Good Morning America.* In December 2009, ABC paired Roberts with George Stephanopoulos as coanchors. The team of Roberts and Stephanopoulos led *Good Morning America* back to the top of the ratings; the program became the number-one morning show again in April 2012, beating NBC's *Today Show,* which had held the top spot for the previous sixteen years. Roberts was inducted into the Women's Basketball Hall of Fame as part of the Hall of Fame class of 2012 for her contributions to and impact on the game of women's basketball through her broadcasting work and play.

In 2012, Roberts was diagnosed with myelodysplastic syndrome, a disease of the bone marrow. Roberts went public with her illness on *Good Morning America* and received a 2012 Peabody Award for the program. The Peabody citation credits her for "allowing her network to document and build a public service campaign around her battle with the rare disease and inspiring hundreds of potential bone marrow donors to register and heightening awareness of the need for even more donors." In 2013, ESPN awarded its Arthur Ashe Courage Award to Robin Roberts at the 2013 ESPYs.

A list of the top 70 women sportscasters of all time was published. It was however, unfortunate that only four women of color made the list. Jayne Kennedy was the first black women to make the ranking, coming in at number 51. Pam Oliver ranked 59, while Stag Steele ranked 65 and Jemele Hill took the final slot at number 69. According to the author the ranking was solely based on their combined knowledge of sports. In the immortal words of former NFL player and sportscaster Chris Carter, "Man, Come On!"

CHAPTER TEN

The Black Gay Athlete

*"First of all, every player has played with gay guys. It bothers
me when I hear these reporters and jocks get on TV and say,
'Oh, no guy can come out in a team sport. These guys would go
crazy.' First of all, quit telling me what I think. I'd rather have
a gay guy who can play than a straight guy who can't play."*

—Charles Barkley

The masculinity struggles associated with being a black athlete continues
to challenge the black identity. Remember Dennis Rodman, everyone felt
that Dennis was some type of nut case that just happened to play basketball.
He was a cross dressing NBA rebound champ more than once and a five-
time NBA World Champion. Rodman openly admitted to struggling
with his identity, as well as suffering from depression despite being a
multimillion-dollar showman. It is fair to say that Dennis Rodman was
credited with challenging the status quo of masculinity for black athletes.
Rodman constantly challenged the boundaries of black masculinity within
sports. The male black athlete is known for his massive masculine behavior
and attitude both on and off the field. Flash back to May of 1995, when
Dennis Rodman appeared on the cover of Sports Illustrated, the leading
sports publication during the 1990s. It was what Rodman was wearing
that had everyone talking about black masculinity. Here you have a 6' 6"
black athlete with reddish-orange hair, a dog collar around his neck, several

pair of large earrings, hot pants and a sleeveless vest that was similar to a woman's halter top. Rodman was instrumental in pushing the button publicly that challenged the black athletes' masculinity.

Clearly Rodman openly embraced gay culture with his dress and lifestyle off the court. Rodman's style and behavior was completely opposite of the black athlete in general. Many inside and outside of the professional sports world questioned his motives. In addition to embracing gay culture, he also openly expressed interest in the gay lifestyle, which was not an easy pill to digest for the majority of the leagues black heterosexual players. Was Dennis Rodman just another misunderstood black athlete seeking attention with his cross dressing and proclaimed interest in the gay lifestyle? Remember, Rodman was one of the NBA's Detroit Pistons original "Bad Boys" who publicly dated the mega star Madonna. Despite painting his fingernails, wearing dresses, coloring his hair and hanging out in gay clubs, he openly professed to not being gay. In fact, Rodman stated that if he was gay, he was man enough to say that he was indeed gay. What was so interesting about Rodman was that he always kept people guessing about his sexuality on and off the court. According to Rodman, he grew up in a home with all girls. He played dress up with the girls, so crossing dressing, halter tops, lip stick, painted nails, and make-up were all too common. As he stated in his book, *Bad As I Want To Be,* "Mentally, I probably am bisexual based on my behaviors both on and off the court." People thought that Dennis had to be either gay or bisexual; he was instantly accepted in the gay and bisexual communities, where the black athlete entertainers are usually treated somewhat differently than the average entertainer. Gay black entertainers are more likely to be accepted by society than the gay black athlete. It is more of a major tragedy or scandal when a black-athlete publicly comes out of the closet and shows the world that he is openly gay. For the most part, few athletes, let along black athletes, are willing to come out and say that they are gay.

In terms of professional sports, the overall attitude by the majority population is similar to the military: Don't ask, don't tell your sexual orientation. John Amaechi was the first professional basketball player to publicly admit to being gay. However, Amaechi only revealed that he was gay after retiring from the NBA. According to Amaechi, if he had disclosed that he was gay during his playing days, he would have lost his job as an NBA player. Amaechi played college basketball at Penn State before moving on to the NBA where he spent five seasons. In 2007, Amaechi released his book entitled "Man in the Middle." Shortly after his playing career ended, Amaechi joined the ranks of a few brave professional male athletes who publicly shared his sexual orientation and sexual identity, thus questioning the masculinity of the male athlete. According to Amaechi, he knew his sexuality as a young teenager, and kept it hidden all throughout his collegiate days at Penn State and during his short NBA career. Amaechi also believes that there are many other gay players in the NBA today who remain in the closet. Coming out in any professional sport can be a very frightening prospect. The impact could have devastating psychological consequences, not to mention devastating financial consequences. The majority of professional athletes do not believe that any openly gay person could survive in the league of professional sports like football and basketball. Around the NBA league, there are mixed emotions about coming out, staying in the closet, and the issue of truth, which brings one back to the military's "don't ask, don't tell."

In 1977, former NFL player David Kopay came out; offensive lineman Roy Simmons and defensive lineman Esera Tuaolo were the most recent professional football players to come out of the closet. In major league baseball, Glenn Burke came out during the 1970s, and Billy Beam came out after his career ended in the 1990s. Glenn Burke would later die from complications of AIDS in 1995. When the LA Dodgers discovered that Glenn Burke was gay, they ruined his baseball career. The team was not willing to deal with a gay player and sought to distance themselves from such players. If you had a drug or alcohol problem they would work with you; not if you were gay. It is important to note that is true even today. Homophobia in professional sports is very much alive.

The black athlete has truly come a mighty long way in terms integrating professional and amateur sports. The year is 2017, and we are writing and discussing the role and attributes of the black gay male athlete within the context of the professional and amateur ranks. For this discussion, I direct my attention towards Jason Collins, Michael Sam, and Derrick Gordon. Some attention will also be given to other black gay athletes.

Jason Collins, standing nearly 7' tall, made history by becoming the NBA's first openly and actively gay player. He was later followed by the

University of Missouri Michael Sam who went on to become the first openly gay NFL player to be drafted during the 2014 NFL draft by the Saint Louis Rams. Sam would eventually be cut by the Rams, but he quickly landed another opportunity with the Dallas Cowboys. He was signed to the Cowboys practice squad before once again being cut near the middle of the 2014 NFL season. Then there is the youngest of the three, the amateur basketball star from the University of Massachusetts, Derrick Gordon. The starting point guard has helped to rebuild the university's basketball program despite struggling with being a gay athlete in such a masculine sport. Gordon was instrumental in helping his team to a 24–9 overall record, which earned the team a first-round appearance in the NCAA tournament in 2014. Gordon, who stands 6' 3", dreams of playing in the NBA despite his sexuality orientation. In most cases when there is conversation about the black male athlete, the theme is often centered around the intersection between highly competitive and even physically aggressive sporting events such as football and basketball. Furthermore, we often associate black male athletes with physical toughness, strength, speed, and, in some cases, explosiveness. The fact that the black athlete is merely recognized for their masculine strength and speed continues to support the notion that the black athlete is nothing more than a macho hypermasculine black product.

According to Anderson and McCormack, in general black athletes are often perceived as thugs and marginalized by their space within the sports context, despite the impressive gains of the civil rights movement and most recently progress towards gay and lesbian rights. At the end of the day, only a brave few black males have come out publicly about their sexuality orientation. The truth remains that the general public is truly concerned about the sexuality of athletes in general. Now being black offers a different set of variables. The gay athlete in general is still very much marginalized and underrepresented in professional and intercollegiate sports. In particular, the black gay athlete faces continued oppression in the form of racism and homophobia from the dominant culture. McCormack and Anderson also suggest the attitudes of the younger generations have improved in recent years. Collins, Sam, and Gordon all represent a generational and attitudinal shift in the context of sports. Despite the inclusion of a few gay athletes, homophobic views have not been eliminated from sports, nor has the issue of racism. Many heterosexual male athletes both black and white seemingly demonstrate a somewhat softer, loving, and accepting version of masculinity compared to athletes from the 1970s and 1980s.

The Collins Perspective

There was once a big giant by the name of Jason Collins, he stood nearly 7' tall and played the game of basketball. According to Collins "I did not set out to be the first openly gay athlete in a major American team sport, but since I am I am happy to start the conversation" (*Sports Illustrated*, May, 2012). Twelve-year NBA veteran Jason Collins came out as an openly gay NBA player, shocking many in the sports world. Collin's announcement shook up the sports world and made gay-rights history. As now more athletes feel freer to come out about their sexuality and seek equality for other gay athletes. Title IX legislation, passed over forty years ago, provides equal access for women to integrate intercollegiate athletics. At present within the governance of the NCAA inclusion efforts are a top priority. There has been much emphasis and discussion about more inclusion of the Lesbian, Gay, Bisexual, Transgender and Queer (LGBTQ) population within the context of the NCAA and intercollegiate sports. Jason Collins was a member of the NBA's Boston Celtics and the team's center when he informed the sports world that he was gay. At the time of Collins' announcement, he was thirty-four years old. In *Sports Illustrated,* Collins began the interview by saying the following: "I am a thirty-four-year-old NBA center, I'm black and I am gay." After Collins' decision to go public, various discussions have occurred in reference to the role and acceptance of openly gay athletes in professional sports. Discussions about gay athletes continue to be a real framing topic among both men and women in general. One of the major concerns and discussion has been the debate on how gay athletes would affect team chemistry, including potential locker-room problems. Despite a few players openly coming out about being gay, men's professional sports continues to lack a true voice for inclusion and acceptance. Collins was the very first active NBA player to admit that he was gay. According to Collins, the journey of self-discovery and self-acknowledgement began in his hometown of Los Angeles, California, where he and his twin brother earned two state high school championships, one NCAA Final Four appearance, and one Elite Eight NCAA tournament appearance. After separating from his brother, Collins went on to appear in nine NBA playoffs during his twelve years in the NBA. Collins' decision to come out was largely based on a lot of thinking and introspection about who he really was within the context of his basketball journey. The NBA's 2011 lockout greatly aided Collins' decision: Thanks to the lockout, there was a delay in Collins' normal preseason NBA regular routine which ultimately forced Collins to do some soul searching about who he really was and what he really wanted out of life beyond basketball.

During the *Sports Illustrated* interview, Collins shared with the magazine a story about his aunt Teri, a superior court judge in San Francisco. Collins had shared his news with his family prior to opening up to *Sports Illustrated,* and he was shocked to learn that his aunt already knew; in fact, she had known for years and that he was hiding behind the masculine NBA images. His aunt's main concern was what took him so long to admit who he was. According to Collins, it was the support and level of comfort he felt after talking with his family members, particularly his aunt, who helped him to understand it was time to come clean about his sexuality. Collins regrets that it took him some thirty-three years to tell the world in a matter of seconds that he was a black gay man. For years, Collins seemingly struggled with the issue of being a black male, who just happened to be nearly 7' tall and a member of the NBA, which is overrepresented with black masculine and homophobic culture.

According to Collins, for years he always depended on his inner censor button about his sexuality, until that day when his censor button refused to respond. At that point, he knew the timing was right, so he did what he should have done several years prior. Collins' ability to finally ignore his inner censor button ultimately resulted in his decision to come out and be openly gay despite the fallout. For Collins, it was not just about the fact that he was gay; it was more about the fact that he was a black gay NBA player. If Collins were white or foreign, would such a public debate or discussion ensue about the first active and openly gay man in a league that is based largely on the culture of masculinity, physical abilities, and aggressive style? The attitudes of nongay athletes in the locker room can be a very challenging and even frightening. This further denies gay athletes a safe avenue through which they can openly express themselves and feel free to be who they really are within the contexts of such a masculine sports culture where nongays continue to behave in a manner that openly discriminates against the gay lifestyle.

The Sam Perspective

Then there was Michael Sam, college standout at the University of Missouri and a star in the Southeastern Conference, arguably the toughest and most competitive football conference in the land. Sam was the 2013 Co-SEC defensive player of the year who somehow effectively managed his masculine toughness and physical aggression on the football field, while maintaining his intimate feminine side, including his emotions and feelings. Sam grew up in a small southeast Texas town called Hitchcock. To say that football may have just saved Sam's life is an understatement. Sam's childhood was nothing short of horrifying. Sam was the seventh of eight children, and the youngest son in the family. The family was known throughout the town as "those damn Sams." In fact, Sam's eldest sister died before he was even born, she was accidentally knocked off a dock and drowned at only two years old. Shortly thereafter, his teenage brother, Russell, was shot dead trying to break into someone's home. Three years later, he and his younger sister were the last to see his brother Julian before he walked away from the family home one day and never returned. The local police described Julian a missing person, but the case was never solved. The remaining brothers, Josh and Chris, were in and out of jail and routinely beat their youngest brother for failing to follow in their footsteps. Chris is currently serving thirty years for aggravated robbery. Sam would eventually spend a percentage of his elementary-school years living with his mother in a car. His mother was a devoted Jehovah's Witness and she insisted that he not be involved in any form of organized sports. However, Sam insisted otherwise. It was during Sam's junior year in high school that one of Sam's coaches suggested he was talented enough to play Division I football, which opened the door of opportunity at the University of Missouri.

Sam starred at the University of Missouri as a football player, where he met his boyfriend Vito Cammisano also a student-athlete on the swim team. The relationship between Sam and Cammisano became a subject of intense media speculation after the couple was captured on camera sharing an intimate kiss in celebration of Sam being drafted by the Saint Louis Rams. Sam credits Cammisano with helping him to be more at peace and comfortable with being gay. Sam's teammates at Missouri were more than supported of his lifestyle off the field. They were even more proud of his decision to come out and speak out publicly about being a black gay athlete. Just prior to the start of the 2013 season, Sam publicly announced his sexuality, thus making history, as he became the first openly gay college football player. Sam recalls the actual date that he addressed his teammates at Missouri.

Sam recalled that when he told the team that he was gay, it was the first time that he had ever told anyone other than himself. Sam indicated that he was extremely nervous, but his teammates were very understanding and supportive. On the field, Sam came to play, earning himself SEC co-defensive player of the year. Sam never showed any signs of weakness in his game as he helped Missouri earn an NCAA bowl appearance and the SEC championship game against Auburn University. Within the world of intercollegiate athletics, Sam has gained the respect and attention of many nonbelievers that a gay man could excel in a nongay sport like football. Sam was focused and determined to make all nonbelievers true believes. According to Sam, just because you are gay, you can still participate and have an impact in a highly competitive and aggressive sport like football.

By the time Michael Sam had officially come out publicly, believe it or not, things actually become even more complicated. Sam told his teammates in August, but it was not until February of 2014 that he actually went public. The process of coming out was initiated by his sports agent and shepherded by publicists Howard Bragman and Cyd Zeigler. The pair combined their media experience and years of gay-rights advocacy to provide Sam with a powerhouse plan to capture the appropriate media coverage that would not diminish the athletic abilities of their client despite his being an openly gay black man hoping to play with the NFL.

Bragman and Zeigler worked extremely hard and established the timeline and selected the place for Sam's coming-out announcement. In the end, they decided on the front page of the New York Times to publicly announce to the world that Michael Sam was indeed gay, but he still wants to continue playing football as a member of the NFL. Bragman and Zeigler then worked hard to prepare Sam for the tough questioning that he was sure to face in the coming weeks. Zeigler put Sam through a series of intense mock interviews that centered around being a gay NFL prospect who could really present himself well and articulately in front of the camera while answering the tough questions that he would surly encounter from the various media outlets, sports writers, coaches, and general managers. Overall Bragman and Zeigler did a good job managing his announcement, but they received a questionable grade for the weak involvement of actual LGBTQ organizations. Establishing Sam's presence with the LGBTQ organizations and their progressive movements would have provided a new perspective in terms gender equality in sports by showing the world that a gay man can play an aggressive and competitive sport like football while championing the efforts of the LGBTQ community. It was unfortunate that the LGBTQ community organizations were not invited to Sam's coming-out announcement. In fact, they reported feeling disrespected and in the dark about Sam's coming-out announcement. After all, he was now a part of their inner circle. They felt that they should have been included in this significant historic announcement.

The Gordon Perspective

The youngest of the pack, Derrick Gordon, a 6'-3" point guard at the University of Massachusetts, also made history as he become the nation's first openly gay NCAA Division I college basketball player. Since announcing his sexual orientation to the public, Gordon reported that he now really feels free to fully embrace his new life as an openly gay black intercollegiate student-athlete. Along Gordon's journey of self-discovery, he has now become a spokesman for the LGBTQ community. Those closest to Gordon have also reported a more free-spirited Gordon since his announcement. For Gordon, coming out seems to have taken a lot of pressure off him; even his teammates and head coach seemed to recognize a positive and more outgoing free-will attitude in Gordon. They all believe that Gordon is more comfortable in his skin now that the world knows that he is openly gay.

Gordon will definitely not be the first, nor the last, to admit that life was more difficult when he was hiding his true sexual lifestyle and preference. Now that it is out of the bag, his coaches and teammates see Gordon as a much happier person both on and off the court. According to coaches and teammates, Gordon now smiles more than ever. It is important to note that coming out to the world took a tremendous amount of courage. His teammates have all rallied behind him since he went public. One of Gordon's teammates reported that, prior to his big announcement, Gordon was somewhat isolated from his teammates off the court and it was like he was not really a part of the team. Now things are completely different for Gordon; his relationship with his teammates and coaches is now on a new level. Gordon has been tremendously positive and outgoing. He has support and love from his teammates despite his sexual orientation. Similar to Sam, Gordon also dreams of playing professional basketball in the NBA after college. Gordon frequently consults with Michael Sam and Jason Collins for advice and support. Gordon has also become something of an ambassador for the LGBTQ community. At the end of the day, Gordon seems blessed to have the support and backing of his family, teammates, and coaches; it all helps to fuel his power and success on and off the court.

Prior to Gordon's, Sam's, and Collin's coming out, there had been a slight decline in the homophobic attitudes and beliefs of many younger people. Research conducted by McCormack suggests that now more than any time heterosexual male students are, in general, more inclusive of their gay peers, and many are even proud of their progay stance. McCormack further suggests that being gay today does not automatically negatively impacts a person's popularity, but being openly homophobic does. The overall declining significance of homophobic attitudes reveal that young people early on tend to develop real meaningful and living friendships across many social groups, including straight and gay individuals. McCormack argues that, at the end of the day, toughness and aggression has been replaced with emotional intimacy and even a willingness to openly display affection toward those who may have a different sexuality. In most recent times, there has been a definite generational shift, whereby young boys are now free to speak out about feminizing activities without being censured or fearing social marginalization. Following in the footsteps of Michael Sam, Gordon gathered a powerhouse team to help make his announcement.

He consulted with and hired Wade Davis, a former NFL player who just happens to be openly gay himself. Davis is executive director of "You Can Play," an advocacy group for gay athletes.

According to Gordon, his final decision to come out was inspired by Michael Sam's decision to tell his teammates at Missouri. Gordon had tremendous support and encouragement throughout the process. He consulted with Wade Davis to work closely with members of the LGBTQ community and Anthony Nicodemo, a high school basketball coach from Yonkers, New York. Nicodemo also just recently came out as being gay himself and is a member of the LGBTQ sports coalition that advocates for the gay athletes. Wade Davis felt that, from a basketball perspective, Nicodemo's experience as coach and former basketball player could lend Gordon some help. Gordon and Nicodemo spent considerable time together prior the formal announcement: watching basketball games, analyzing players, and even discussing how he was going to share with the world of intercollegiate athletics that he was gay and proud of his status.

For nearly a year, Gordon and Nicodemo meet weekly to plan strategies for the naysayers and world of nongay athletes who might object and oppose his decision to go public. Nicodemo's efforts helped Gordon feel comfortable enough to share the news with his parents before telling is teammates. Just like his teammates, Gordon's parents were 100% on board from day one, which was somewhat shocking for Gordon at first. He did admit that he was concerned about how those closest to him would react. He was also concerned about the reactions of basketball fans and other players that he would play against. Gordon is a very comfortable and competent point guard who is the emotional leader of the UMass Minutemen basketball team. Gordon averaged nearly ten points per game in 2014, helping the team reach first round of the NCAA tournament. As Gordon prepares for his final season at UMass, he continues to dream of playing in the NBA next. Sam's and Gordon's coming out parties were both well-planned and effectively managed media events. Both were scripted and choreographed to ensure that general public would receive a fair and earnest story about their sexual orientation and identity.

EPILOGUE

In this his book project I offer the reader a greater insight into the black athlete's psyche. The book presents the significant challenges of racist and oppressive actions that black athletes continue to face today. I hope that this book serves as a reminder of W.E.B Du Bois' essay, "The Souls of Black Folk," which focuses on racism and oppression at the dawn of the twentieth century. I am hopeful that this book will challenge the reader to consider the varying degrees of racism and oppression in the world of sports both past and present. Even W.E.B Du Bois would not have predicted, over a century ago, that organized sports involving blacks would emerge into such a noteworthy industry, producing millionaire black athletes yet still bounded in such a race-based and oppressive America.

This book takes a more contemporary look at the plight of the black athlete, while also putting into perspective the historical struggles of racism and oppression experienced by the black athlete in America. During the 1950s and 1960s members of black communities were fighting for basic civil and human rights in America. They wanted the opportunity to attend schools, ride buses, drink from public water fountains, and the ability to vote. Then came desegregation and integration which allowed a few black athletes opportunity to integrate the once segregated world of athletics. Over the years, we have witness the opening of the flood gate, as other black athletes all throughout the United States are now playing the games they so love before large numbers of nonblack fans. Despite all of the opportunities afforded the black athlete today, the real question still remains, have blacks athletes collectively been given less than their equal share for their loyalty to America.

The valuable history lesson taught to us by John Carlos and Tommy

Smith during the 1968 Olympic Games in Mexico City is one that we must still reflect upon. The moment was an epic one, where two black athletes pulled off a silent political demonstration for the world to witness. Both Carlos and Smith raised their black gloves in the form of a fist in the air and kept them raised until the anthem had finished. Still today, people are talking about the social political actions of Carlos and Smith. Now let us fast forward to the present day, we now have two modern day black athletes advancing their political protest focusing once again on the human rights of the poor marginalized communities in America (poor blacks). We are truly blessed to have Colin Kaepernick and Eric Reid advocating and fighting for rights of those who are unable to fight or speak for themselves. It appears that Kaepernick and Reid might just be the one-two punch to the address the NFL modern day slavery issues and some of the social injustice that continue to handicapped poor people of color.

Colin Kaepernick, Eric Reid and LeBron James are all examples of a new generation of black liberated athletes. They are seemingly very much vested in the awakening of not just the black athlete, but the entire black community. They are more concerned about their ancestry history, the future their people than getting a check. It really takes a special kind of person to be so committed and dedicated to ensuring that the path for opportunities are clear for people of color in America. They all share so much concerns and compassion for their people who have endured hundreds of years of oppression in a country that still to this day does not place high value on people of color unless that are providing some value to them in term of service. Colin Kaepernick, Eric Reid and LeBron James you are indeed the new generation black athlete hero.

The goals and objectives of this book were to assemble a collection of chapters that would enrich the readers' appetite about the psychology of sports in America dating back to the arrival of Africans to American. This book serves as a reference point of advocating for the black athlete social and emotional development. There should be a serious advocacy effort in place for the current and future black athlete. This book was written as part hyper-sports sociology and psychology history book with a flare of the past, coupled with current movements in both professionally and collegiate sports.

BIBLIOGRAPHY

Anderson, Eric, and Mark McCormack. 2014. Being a Black Gay Male Athlete, *Gender & Society,* May.

Hattery, Angela J., and Earl Smith. 2017. The Unconditional Love and Exploitation of the Black Male Athlete. *Gender & Society,* February.

Armour, Nancy. 2014. "Shame Can't Be Shifted." *USA Today Sports,* May, 14.

————. 2014. "NFL Needs to Speed up on New Policy." *USA Today Sports,* November 12.

Badenhausen, K. 2014. "As Stern Says Goodbye, Knicks, Lakers Set Records As NBA's Most Valuable Teams." *Forbes,* January 22. http://www.forbes.com/sites/kurtbadenhausen/2014/01/22/as-stern-says-goodbye-knicks-lakers-set-records-as-nbas-most-valuable-teams/#11d8c965b88b (accessed June 15, 2014).

Baker, William J. 1986. *Jesse Owens: An American Life.* New York: The Free Press.

Bell, Jarrett. 2014. "Study: Diversity Plunges in NFL." *USA Today Sports,* May 2.

Berkowitz, Steve. 2015. "NCAA Nearly Topped $1 Billion in Revenue in 2014." *USA Today Sports,* March 11. http://www.usatoday.com/story/sports/college/2015/03/11/ncaa-financial-statement-2014-1-billion-revenue/70161386 (accessed March 16, 2017).

Betts, Richard J. 1974. *America's Sporting Heritage: 1850–1950.* Reading, MA: Addison-Wesley.

Bhagat, Mihir. 2010. *Do Professional Athletes Get Paid Too Much Money?* http://bleacherreport.com/articles/366795-do-athletes-get-paid-too-much-money (accessed March 16, 2017).

Bhasin, K. 2011. "13 Shocking Stats That Show How NCAA Schools Are Failing at Diversity." *Business Insider,* April 27. http://www. businessinsider.com/ncaa-diversity-facts-2011-4 (accessed January 12, 2017).

Brandt, D. 2014. "Money Woes, Declining Talent Plague HBCU Football." *USA Today Sports,* May 26. http://www.usatoday.com/story/ sports/ncaaf/2014/05/26/money-woes-declining-talent-plague-hbcu-football/9597123/ (accessed January 12, 2017).

Brennan, Christine. 2014. "Church Sends Wrong Message." *USA Today Sports,* May 2, 2014.

Coakley, Jay S. 1990. *Sports in Society: Issues and Controversies,* 4th ed. St. Louis, MO: Times Mirror/Mosby College.

Cortés, C. E. 2013. "Racial Report Card." In *Multicultural America: A Multimedia Encyclopedia* (pp. 2003–2005). Thousand Oaks, CA: Sage.

Deford, F. 2013. "NCAA Should 'Bolster And Reinforce' African-American Players." *National Public Radio,* July 23. http://www. npr.org/2013/07/24/204837926/ncaa-should-bolster-and-reinforce-african-american-players (accessed June 12, 2014).

Demas, L. 2010. *Integrating the Gridiron: Black Civil Rights and American College Football.* New Brunswick, NJ: Rutgers University Press.

Edwards, Harry. 1969. *The Revolt of the Black Athlete.* New York: Free Press.

———. 1973. *Sociology of Sport.* Homewood, IL: Dorsey Press.

———. 1979. *Black Students.* New York: Free Press.

Eisen, George, and David K. Wiggins, eds. 1994. *Ethnicity and Sport in North American History and Culture.* Westport, CT: Greenwood.

Ford, Richard Thompson. 2008. "Blackballed: Why are there are so few black coaches in college football?" *Slate,* December 26. http:// www.slate.com/articles/sports/sports_nut/2008/12/blackballed.html (accessed March 16, 2017).

Foreman, Thomas E. 1957. *Discrimination Against the Negro in American Athletics, A Thesis.* Fresno, CA: Rand Research Associates.

Glesson, Scott. 2014. "UMASS Gordon Done Hiding." *USA Today,* November 11.

Griffith, Jon. 2010. "Sports in Shackles: The Athletic and Recreational Habits of Slaves on Southern Plantations." *Chapman University Historical Review* 2, no. 2: 59–79.

Grossman, Evan. 2014. "The Lowest Paid Athletes in All of Professional Sports." *Men's Journal,* November 25. http://www.mensjournal.com/adventure/races-sports/the-lowest-paid-athletes-in-all-of-professional-sports-20141125 (accessed March 16, 2017).

Grudman, Adolf H. 1986. "The Image of Intercollegiate Sports and the Civil Rights Movement: A Historian's View." In *Fractured Focus: Sport as a Reflection of Society,* edited by Richard E. Lapchick, 77–85. Lexington, MA: Lexington Books.

Harper, S. R., C. D. Williams, Jr., & H. W. Blackman. 2013. *Black Male Student-Athletes and Racial Inequities in NCAA Division I College Sports.* Center for the Study of Race & Equity in Education. https://www.gse.upenn.edu/equity/sites/gse.upenn.edu.equity/files/publications/Harper_Williams_and_Blackman_%282013%29.pdf (accessed June 13, 2014).

Harris, Othello. 1993. "African-American Predominance in Collegiate Sport." In *Racism in College Athletics,* edited by Dana Brooks and Ronald Althouse, 51–74. Morgantown, WV: Fitness Informational Technology.

Henderson, K. 1947. *Ball, Bat, and Bishop: The Origin of Ball Games.* New York: Rockport Press.

Hinton, Ed, Earnest Reese, and David Davidson. 1986. "Run for Respect: A Study of Black Football Players and the South." *Atlanta Journal Constitution,* September 7–14, pp. C1–12.

Hoberman, John M. 1997. *Darwin's Athletes: How Sport Has Damaged Black America and Preserved the Myth of Race.* New York: Mariner Books.

———. 2000. "The Price of 'Black Dominance.'" *Society* 37, no. 3: 49–56.

Horrow, Rick, and Karla Swatek. 2011. "The 3Ms of March Madness: Money, Marketing, Media." *Business Week,* March 17. https://www.bloomberg.com/news/articles/2011-03-17/the-3ms-of-march-madness-money-marketing-media (accessed June 13, 2014).

Jones, James Charles. 1971. *A Study of Black Students in Integrated Universities Compared with their Counterparts in Black Universities* (Ph.D. dissertation). Michigan State University.

King, W. 1995. *Stolen Childhood: Slave Youth in Nineteenth-Century America.* Bloomington: Indiana University Press.

Klopman, M. 2011, March 15. "Adrian Peterson: NFL Like 'Modern Day Slavery.'" *Huffington Post.* http://www.huffingtonpost.com/2011/03/15/adrian-peterson-slavery-nfl_n_836090.html (accessed June 15, 2014).

McCormack, Mark. 2012. *The declining significance of homophobia.* Oxford, England: Oxford University Press.

Maguire, Joseph Anthony, William N. Thompson, Allen Guttmann, and David C. Rowe. 2015. "Traditional African Sports." *Encyclopedia Britannica.* http://www.britannica.com/EBchecked/topic/561041/sports/253548/Traditional-African-sports (accessed January 12, 2017).

Martin, C. H. 2010. *Benching Jim Crow: The Rise and Fall of the Color Line in Southern College Sports, 1890–1980.* Urbana: University of Illinois Press.

Morrision, David. 2014. "Rams Welcome Sam." *USA Today Sports,* May 14.

Myerberg, Paul. 2014. "Early-Exit Turnstile Turns Even Faster: Non-Seniors in NFL Draft; 91 and Counting," *USA Today Sports,* January 15.

Nagi, Kelly. 2013. "Grambling Responds to Concerns." *ESPN,* October 20. http://www.espn.com/college-football/story/_/id/9846943/grambling-state-tigers-players-send-letter-complaint-administration (accessed March 16, 2017).

Nobles, Marko. 2013. "Harlem Week: Players from Historically Black Colleges and Universities Have Gone on to Have "Super" Careers in NFL." *NY Daily News,* August 6. http://www.nydailynews.com/new-york/uptown/harlem-week-black-colleges-nfl-best-super-men-article-1.1417343 (accessed June 14, 2014).

Owens, Leslie H. 1977. *This Species of Property: Slave Life and Culture in the Old South.* New York: Oxford University Press.

Paulson, Ken. 2014. "Isn't Michael Sam Tweet Free Speech?" *USA Today,* May 14.

Perry, Andre. 2014. "Black Athletes Must Pick up the Ball on Graduation Rates." *Hechinger Report,* January 6. http://hechingerreport.org/content/black-athletes-must-pick-up-the-ball-on-graduation-rates_14363/ (accessed June 13, 2014).

Peterson, Marvin W. 1972. *Black Students at White Universities.* New York: Praeger.

Powell, S. 2008. *Souled Out: How Blacks Are Winning and Losing in Sports.* Champaign, IL: Human Kinetics.

Rawley, J. A. 1981. *The Transatlantic Slave Trade: A History.* New York: Norton.

Rhoden, William C. 1989. "Many Black College Athletes Express Feelings of Isolation." *NY Times,* April 5. http://www.nytimes.com/1989/04/06/sports/many-black-college-athletes-express-feelings-of-isolation.html (accessed June 13, 2014).

———. 2006. *Forty Million Dollar Slaves: The Rise, Fall, and Redemption of the Black Athlete.* New York: Crown.

Roberts, John. M., Malcolm J. Arthur, and Robert B. Bush. 1959. "Games in Culture." *American Anthropologist* 61, no. 4: 597–605.

Roberts, Randy. 1983. *Papa Jack: Jack Johnson and the Era of White Hopes,* New York: Free Press.

Rolett, Burl. 2014. March Madness teams compete for share of $200 million. *Richmond BizSense,* March 21. http://richmondbizsense.com/2014/03/21/march-madness-math-can-get-fuzzy (accessed March 16, 2017).

Rovell, Darren. 2013. "NCAA Holds Firm: No Pay for Play." *ESPN,* December 11. http://espn.go.com/college-sports/story/_/id/10119750/ncaa-president-mark-emmert-insists-pay-play-model-coming (accessed June 14, 2014).

Rust, Edna, and Art Rust, Jr. 1978. *Joe Louis: My Life.* New York: Harcourt Brace Jovanovich.

———. 1985. *Art Rust's Illustrated History of the Black Athlete.* Garden City, NY: Doubleday.

Sammons, Jeffery T. 1994. "Race and Sport: A Critical, Historical Examination. *Journal of Sport History* 21, no. 3: 203–78.

Schroeder, George. 2014. "NCAA Big Wheels Spinning." *USA Today Sports,* May 14.

———. 2014. "NCAA Gears up for Division I Power Shift." *USA Today Sports,* January 15.

Schwartz, Nick. 2013. "The Average Career Earnings of Athletes across America's Major Sports Will Shock You." *USA Today,* October 24. http://ftw.usatoday.com/2013/10/average-career-earnings-nfl-nba-mlb-nhl-mls (accessed March 16, 2017).

Shannon, Ryan. 2015. "Recent Firings Sound Alarms for Black College Basketball Coaches." *Chicago Tribune,* April 1. http://www.chicagotribune.com/sports/college/ct-black-coaches-ncaa-spt-0402-20150401-story.html (accessed March 16, 2017).

Smith, Thomas G. 1988. "Outside the Pale: The Exclusion of Blacks from the National Football League, 1934–1946." *Journal of Sports History* 15, no. 3: 255–81.

Spivey, Donald. 1988. "End Jim Crow in Sports: The Protest at New York University, 1940–1941." *Journal of Sports History* 15, no. 3: 282–303.

Sports Illustrated, May, 2012.

Taylor, P. 2008. "The Color of Money." *Sports Illustrated,* July 7. http://www.si.com/vault/2008/07/07/105709330/the-color-of-money (accessed June 12, 2014).

Wiggins, David K. 1979. *Sport and Popular Pastimes in the Plantation Community: The Experience* (Ph.D, diss.). University of Maryland.

———. 1988. "'The Future of College Athletics Is at Stake:' Black Athletes and Racial Turmoil on Three Predominantly White University Campuses, 1968–1972." *Journal of Sports History* 15, no. 3: 304–33.

———. 1997. *Glory Bound Back Athletes in White America.* Syracuse, NY: Syracuse University Press.

———. 1993. "Critical Events Affecting Racism in Athletics." *The African-American Athlete's Experience,* In *Racism in College Athletics,* edited by Dana Brooks and Ronald Althouse, 15–36. Morgantown, WV: Fitness Informational Technology.

Wyche, Steve. 2008. "Ernie Davis' Legacy Lives on Long after His Death." http://www.nfl.com/news/story/09000d5d80b75df1/article/ernie-davis-legacy-lives-on-long-after-his-death (accessed June 13, 2014).

ABOUT THE AUTHOR

In an era when black-athletes are commonly compared to African slaves, Dr. Pinckney draws a connection between William Rhoden's *Forty Million Dollar Slaves* and Harry Edwards' earlier work about black-athletes' integration and segregation issues. This book chronicles the past and current history of blacks in sports. It reads like a hybrid: part history, part sociology, and part current issues. Dr. Pinckney captures the rise and slow decline of segregation in college and professional athletics. He examines socially and politically imposed policies of racism and explains the social forces that eventually forced blacks and historically black colleges and universities to accept second-class segregated competition.

Dr. Pinckney devotes special attention to the slaves and life on southern plantations. He further explores the changing social attitudes and the sociocultural factors associated with sporting competition that turned the tide and allowed the recruitment of black-athletes and hiring of a few black coaches. This book also takes a close look at the academic problem in intercollegiate athletics and financial issues facing historically black colleges and universities. Dr. Pinckney skillfully weaves existing arguments and documentation about the black gay athlete, and the role black women played in the integration of sports as not only athletes, but sportscasters. Dr. Pinckney also includes a chapter devoted to three pioneers who broke racial barriers and opened the doors for other blacks to enter. He also takes into account the conscious effects of racism and discrimination in both the past and the present.

Dr. Charles Pinckney is a faculty member at the University of North Carolina at Charlotte and at Livingstone College, as well as NCAA Faculty Athletic Representative and a former member of the NCAA Division II

Legislative Committee. He has authored articles, coauthored book chapters, and presented at various conferences. Dr. Pinckney is NCAA FARA Fellow and has worked extensively to improve the academic success rates of black student-athletes. He is currently president of the Central Intercollegiate Athletic Association Faculty Athletic Representative Association, whereby he champions academic success and advancing awareness of student-athletes mental health and wellbeing policies that will enhance the twelve member institutions. The Central Intercollegiate Athletic Association is recognized as a conference that serves historically black colleges and universities in North Carolina, Virginia, Maryland, and Pennsylvania. Dr. Pinckney teaches the following courses: Sports Psychology, Psychology of the Black Experience, Introduction to Hip-Hop Culture, Global Hip-Hop Culture and Hip-Hop Culture and Entrepreneurship.